BATTLE YOUR BANK— AND WIN!

BATTLE YOUR BANK— AND WIN!

Edward F. Mrkvicka, Jr.

William Morrow and Company, Inc. • New York

This book presents the author's opinions on the subject of consumer banking. The author does not intend to render legal, accounting, or other professional service by presenting these opinions. The author and publisher specifically disclaim responsibility for loss or risk incurred as a consequence of the application of any advice or information presented here.

Library of Congress Cataloging in Publication Data
Mrkvicka, Edward F.
    Battle your bank—and win!

    Includes index.
    1. Banks and banking—United States.   2. Finance, Personal.   I. Title.
HG2491.M74   1984   332.024   84-4648
ISBN 0-688-03952-9

Printed in the United States of America

First Edition

1 2 3 4 5 6 7 8 9 10

BOOK DESIGN BY RICHARD ORIOLO

ACKNOWLEDGMENTS

After more than a decade of being a banker I realized that the enjoyment of helping people was being replaced by the dictates of those in the industry who believed in profits at all costs. Banks are chartered by the government to service the community, and it is hoped that in the attainment of that honorable goal the bank will generate profits. They are not, as modern bankers believe, chartered to make money with the hope that the bank services the community in the process. Banks, like all service institutions, owe their very existence to the customer. It is because they have forgotten this that this book is necessary.

I owe a debt to Frank Malgrande, who helped direct my efforts in the technical process that culminated in this book becoming a reality. Without his help and assistance my goal of helping you cope with your bank might never have been realized.

I am thankful to my parents, Edward, Sr. (Babe), and Ruth, for more than I could possibly acknowledge here, but above all for their unquestioning devotion and love. They taught me, by example, the value of the Ten Commandments, and if they hadn't been chosen as my parents I would have chosen them as my friends.

I am grateful to my in-laws, Bob and Helen Rimnac, for being so dear and for always being there when we've needed them—which has been often.

I am thankful to my sister, Lynn, and my brother, John, for being so much more to me than just my sister and brother. They are truly special people.

Most of all I am thankful to God for the opportunity of life and his very special gifts—our children, Eddie and Kelly.

This book is dedicated to my wife, Maddy, who makes my life worth living. She has always been a beacon of hope and when I get discouraged she reminds me through action or word that the truth *is* worth fighting for. She is a beautiful person who makes my life richer than I ever had a right to expect.

CONTENTS

Contents

INTRODUCTION

I have written this book for one reason: Your bank has been taking advantage of you long enough. It's time for you to fight back and beat the bankers at their own game. To do so successfully, you need ammunition, and that is what this book will give you.

Banks accept your deposits, pay you interest, and then lend you and other customers the same funds at a higher rate than the interest being paid to you by the bank. The difference between these two rates is the bank's profit. Although banks are essential to the financial well-being of the country's entire monetary system, the method of dealing with individual customers on a day-to-day basis is one of legalized theft. It is, of course, crucial for a bank to make an adequate profit, but to accomplish this, the banking system depends on lack of financial knowledge and sophistication of its customers. In the following chapters I will show you how banks accomplish their goals by taking advantage of you, and do it using your own money. I'm also going to show you how you can *effectively fight back.*

Most financial books are unlike this one. I am going to give you the straight facts, and a system to beat the system. This isn't one of those books that boasts "how to earn $100,000 in ninety days." I have no respect for those books, and in my opinion they are worthless. They take advantage of people who can ill afford their empty promises. And this isn't one of those book with titles such as *The Converse Statistical Trend Curve to Financial Security,* which requires a Ph.D. in economics to understand. This book is simply going to give you a step-by-step approach to saving money while dealing with an institution we all need for one reason or another: the bank. In addition, I have some ideas that not only will *save* you money but will actually *earn* you extra money. That you can save money on banking is an idea that may never have occurred to you.

This book promises straight talk and straight answers. Not necessarily a new approach, but one that certainly has been prostituted by the fast-talking, double-shuffling, deceptive money managers we call bankers. Over the years banks have cultivated a highly respectable image—*one they most certainly don't deserve.* In a sense, you're much better off dealing with a dishonest used-car dealer than with your banker. At least with the used car you are on your guard against being cheated. But the banker has you so confused that you're grateful simply to make a withdrawal successfully, or be allowed to borrow your money back at 10 percent more than the bank is paying you in interest on your deposits. Remember: Bankers thrive on your confusion. Furthermore, bankers can, with the upright image they have created, intimidate you to the point that you abandon common sense. What is the result? You guessed it: You've been had once again. But take heart. Once you know the system, you will find that the average bank officer will be not nearly so intimidating. *At this point the tables are turned.*

It is not my primary purpose to denigrate banks and bankers. It is important, however, to understand the banking system in order to get what you deserve from it. Unfortunately, the system is not fair—it is set up, legally, to allow banks to rip you off. The sharper the banker, the more skilled he or she is in using the system, the more it will cost you and your family to do business with him or her.

As much as possible, I will try to stay away from technical bank jargon except where knowledge of certain terms is required to understand the specific approach recommended in saving money on banking. Implementation of some of my recommendations will take considerable discipline on your part and in a few select situations will require you not to reveal all you know and/or shade the truth to accomplish a goal. Don't let this bother you—your banker tells some real whoppers!

Now for some personal history. I was a professional banker for six years before I became the president of a national bank at thirty-one. I left the banking profession to pursue other opportunities. This book is not intended as an exposé of banking by a disenchanted former member of the club. Rather, I have wanted for many years to inform the public of the flaws in the banking system. But I made the mistake of trying to accomplish this while being part of the system myself. As a result, I have had numerous battles with the Comptroller of the Currency's office in Washington, D.C. Undaunted, I proceeded to write a number of antibanking system articles for various trade journals. The thrust of my attack has always been that banks in general are mismanaged and the system as a whole is not functioning in the best interest of the consumer. In my mind, it doesn't matter if you are robbed of $100 at gunpoint, or if your local banker double-talks you out of $100 in a loan arrangement. In either case, the result is the same: You're out $100. That he wears a pinstriped suit doesn't mean that your banker won't steal from you. Actually, I'm not sure it's the banker's fault—the banking system is set up in a certain way, and bankers behave according to the rules of the system. At any rate, I have come to the conclusion that the system will not change in the foreseeable future. Consequently, I have changed my point of attack. If the system can't be changed, then let's *beat the system,* and while we're at it, let's make a few bucks for ourselves. You are now on your way!

PART I

1

INSTALLMENT LOANS

Since we all need to borrow on occasion, and since it can be a very expensive proposition, this is a good place to start saving money. Not many of us have $9,000 to pay cash for a new car, or $100,000 to pay for a home. Before going into specific lending needs (and here's the first area in which you will have to practice self-discipline), *you should NEVER borrow for a depreciating asset* (an asset that loses value as time elapses) that is not a necessity. (Cars are exceptions, since they generally are necessities.) If you can't pay cash for that color TV, or washer and dryer, save your money until you can. The reason for this becomes evident if we look at the following example:

Cost of television	$650.00
Down payment	− 100.00
Amount financed	550.00
Typical bank finance charge for 24 months	103.93
Total actually paid	$753.93

There is no reason to agree to pay $753.93 for a television set that was probably overpriced at the original price of

$650.00. In addition, that television set, the moment it is delivered to you, is worth (in resale value) approximately half its original purchase price. In short, you now have an asset worth about $325.00 (if you could sell it immediately, which is doubtful), and you still owe $653.93 (the total due over the period of the loan minus your down payment). Not a very good way to build your net worth, is it? NEVER—and I can't stress this enough—buy anything except a necessity on an installment basis. Over the course of your lifetime, this practice alone could save you thousands of dollars. Now let's get to those items for which you absolutely need to borrow.

Suppose you want to take out a car loan. The car has a purchase price of $9,000.00, and you put down $2,000.00 in cash while borrowing the remaining $7,000.00 from the bank. Incidentally, *never let the car dealer arrange your financing.* Although this may be very convenient for you, it adds greatly to your ultimate cost because the bank pays the dealer a rebate, or "kickback," that may amount to as much as 1.5 percent of the total loan. This, of course, is added to your loan repayment. In dollars and cents that could add up to $461.38 in our example loan. Arrange your own financing, even if you have to go to a neighboring state to do it. You'll still be ahead.

Sample Car Loan at 16.79% Annual Percentage Rate for 48 Months

Principal	$7,000.00
Credit life	275.87
Disability insurance	413.81
Amount financed	7,689.68
Finance charge	2,920.72
Total due	10,610.40
Monthly payments	221.05

Note that the total cost exceeds the value of the car by $1,610.40. (That sounds familiar, doesn't it?) At any rate, it can't be helped, you say . . . or can it? How can we improve this drain on your family's finances? First, NEVER agree to credit life insurance and/or disability insurance. I'll get to this more specifically in the next chapter.

Since installment lending is based on a percentage rate times the *original balance,* you are still paying the full rate of interest even though at the twenty-four-month point you have paid back half the money. The bank turns around and lends that money to some other customer, and the net effect is that an aggressive bank can pyramid its money into interest rates that are astronomical when added together. Why should you be paying a rate of interest on $7,000.00 when at the twenty-four-month payment you only owe $3,500.00? The answer is obvious: *You shouldn't!* Now let's see how we can turn this situation around in our favor.

When you go in to talk with your banker about an installment loan, first arrange for him to commit to a specific rate, in this case 16.79 percent. When he drags out the installment loan papers (after the loan approval), tell him you would rather make the loan at the same rate that was just quoted to you, but on a single-payment-note basis for forty-eight months, with monthly payments. Your banker won't like this one bit, as you apparently know something you shouldn't. He will probably try to back out by saying, "Well, we don't make loans like that. All our car loans are on an installment basis." The reason he will most likely attempt to dissuade you is that on a single-payment-note basis you are *charged for only the money you owe at any given time* multiplied by the interest rate, NOT ON THE ORIGINAL BALANCE, as is the case with an installment loan. If he quoted you a rate of 16.79 percent and won't honor that commitment with a note of your choosing, it's time to move all your accounts from that particular bank and seek the loan from another bank. One of the main problems in dealing with a bank is that all things that look equal are not necessarily equal. By law, the bank has the option of selecting different methods of computing interest rates on your deposits (which we will get to later), and unequal note forms and interest computation methods for loans that can drive up your final cost considerably. Let's go back to our car loan example to illustrate my point further. Surely you would agree that 16.79 percent is 16.79 percent no matter how you look at it. Not so.

In our installment loan example, the total interest on the loan was $2,920.72, but I am going to reduce that even further because you remembered not to buy credit life insurance or disability insurance This decreases not only the amount owed but the finance charges as well. The actual interest, without the insurance, would be $2,660.00 on an installment loan basis. Now let's compute the same loan at the same rate on a single-payment note with monthly payments plus interest. Your monthly payments would be $145.83 plus a declining monthly interest charge, as follows:

Payment No.	Balance	Monthly Interest Due	Monthly Payment Amount	Monthly Cash-flow Savings
1	$7,000.00	$97.94	$243.77	(42.52)
2	6,854.17	95.90	241.73	(40.48)
3	6,708.34	93.96	239.69	(38.44)
4	6,562.51	91.82	237.65	(36.40)
5	6,416.68	89.78	235.61	(34.36)
6	6,270.85	87.74	233.57	(32.32)
7	6,125.02	85.70	231.53	(30.28)
8	5,979.19	83.66	229.49	(28.24)
9	5,833.36	81.62	227.45	(26.20)
10	5,687.53	79.58	225.41	(24.16)
11	5,541.70	77.54	223.37	(22.12)
12	5,395.87	75.50	221.33	(20.08)
13	5,250.04	73.46	219.29	(18.04)
14	5,104.21	71.42	217.25	(16.00)
15	4,958.38	69.38	215.21	(13.96)
16	4.812.55	67.34	213.17	(11.92)
17	4,666.72	65.30	211.13	(9.88)
18	4,520.89	63.26	209.09	(7.84)
19	4,375.06	61.22	207.05	(5.80)
20	4,229.23	59.18	205.01	(3.76)
21	4,083.40	57.14	202.97	(1.72)
22	3,937.57	55.10	200.93	.32
23	3,791.74	53.06	198.89	2.36
24	3,645.91	51.02	196.85	4.40
25	3,500.08	48.98	194.81	6.44
26	3,354.25	46.94	192.77	8.48
27	3,208.42	44.90	190.73	10.52

Payment No.	Balance	Monthly Interest Due	Monthly Payment Amount	Monthly Cash-flow Savings
28	3,062.59	42.86	188.69	12.56
29	2,916.76	40.82	186.65	14.60
30	2,770.93	38.78	184.61	16.64
31	2,625.10	36.74	182.57	18.68
32	2,479.27	34.70	180.53	20.72
33	2,333.44	32.66	178.49	22.76
34	2,187.61	30.62	176.45	24.80
35	2,041.78	28.58	174.41	26.84
36	1,895.95	26.54	172.37	28.88
37	1,750.12	24.50	170.33	30.92
38	1,604.29	22.46	168.29	32.96
39	1,458.46	20.41	166.25	35.00
40	1,312.63	18.38	164.21	37.04
41	1,166.80	16.34	162.17	39.08
42	1,020.97	14.30	160.13	41.12
43	875.14	12.26	158.09	43.16
44	729.31	10.22	156.05	45.20
45	583.48	8.18	154.01	47.24
46	437.65	6.14	151.97	49.28
47	291.82	4.10	149.93	51.32
48	145.99	2.06	147.89	53.36
Total interest paid		$2,400.00		

Wait a minute, you say. How can 16.79 percent not be 16.79 percent? The rate is exactly the same in each case. The difference in the amount of interest paid *is the method of interest computation*. This consumer deception, which is perfectly legal, is one of the banker's best income producers.

Let's recap the example loan. First, you didn't buy the credit life insurance or disability insurance, and you insisted on a single-payment note with monthly payments. How much did you save?

Credit life insurance	275.87
Disability insurance	413.81
Cost of financing insurance	262.07
Difference between installment loan and single-payment note	260.00
Total savings	$1,211.75

In reviewing this table, you can see that some interesting financial facts of life have come to light. On the installment basis, your payments were $221.05 throughout the term of the loan. On the single-payment-note basis, *at the same rate,* your payment was $243.77 the first month, $196.85 the twenty-fourth month, and $147.89 the last month. You not only saved a substantial sum of money, but you also improved your monthly cash flow each month as your payments decreased. Granted, it's not a great amount of money each month, and you experience a "loss" through the twenty-first month, but on average it's enough to help take the family out to dinner! The food will taste great. After all, how many times does your banker pick up the tab?

Your banker, of course, won't like this arrangement if he is astute in his profession. This group (astute bankers) fortunately make up only a small percentage of the total banking population. The majority will go along with your requested payment terms because they didn't understand the difference in the first place. It's worth remembering that most senior bank officers achieved their present career level not through hard work and managerial skills. In many cases, they simply outlived the competition. There's an old saying, "I don't want to speak to the person in charge, I want to speak to someone who knows what's going on." When you deal with your bank you want to turn that around. You don't want to talk to someone who knows what's going on, you want to talk to the person in charge, because armed with certain information you can gain the edge you need to make a few bucks. This search for the most incompetent will quite often lead you to the bank president, a person we are going to make *your* friend. You can't afford to be his.

If, by chance, you presently have an installment loan, or ignore my advice and take one out in the future for an item you don't really need, *never pay off the loan in advance.* This only compounds your original error. There is another consumer "deception" in installment lending that is called the Rule of 78s. This is extremely complicated and not necessary to explain here, but simply stated, it is the method by which the bank collects your interest from a specific loan. In short, the bank takes as much of the interest into its profit account as soon as possible. The upshot is that more interest is paid by you the first month than the second, and so on down the line over the course of the payments. Throughout the term of the loan most of the interest is collected during the earlier months and therefore is not rebatable to you if you pay off the loan early. If you pay off an installment loan early, all you have accomplished is to take the exorbitant interest rate the bank charged you originally and add to it the real net cost based on your actual use of the funds. Of course, the best way not to have to worry about the infamous Rule of 78s is not to borrow money on an installment basis in the first place.

CREDIT LIFE AND DISABILITY INSURANCE

Credit life insurance will, in the event of the death of the insured party, pay off the entire outstanding amount of the loan. Disability insurance, in the event you become disabled within the restrictions of the policy's coverage, guarantees your monthly loan payments until you are able to resume work. These insurance policies don't appear all that devious *until* you understand the relationship between the insurance company issuing the insurance, and the bank that receives a fee for acting as the agent or middleman.

To begin with, understand that the *bank* is being insured, not you or your spouse. I can accurately say this even though your family would receive the release from the loan obligation (the loan in its entirety in case of death, or the monthly payments in case of disability). But who actually receives the money? *The bank.* All you accomplished in taking the insurance was to relieve the bank from a collection problem should you die or become ill.

In the case of credit life insurance you are betting the insurance company that you will die before your loan is paid off. The only way you can win is to pass away. That may sound ludicrous, but it's true. For those with a macabre sense of financial security, I suppose this makes sense. It doesn't to me, and it certainly doesn't to the insurance company. To prove my point, ask your banker if he will provide insurance to pay you the entire amount of the loan back if you make all your payments before dying! Banks don't have insurance on loans to cover this because they know they would lose their shirts. Yet that is exactly what they are selling you in reverse, and in the bank's favor. The common practice is that the insurance company pays the bank selling the policy 40 percent of the premium. This return is the same for disability insurance. This means, on our sample loan discussed in the previous chapter, that the bank made an extra $257.87 in premium kickback on a loan that was already structured to take you to the cleaners. If you are absolutely determined to purchase credit life insurance, take a trip to your local insurance agency and arrange a whole life policy for the amount and term of the loan. For example (most insurance companies won't write a policy for less than $10.000.00), I called my local agent using our sample loan, and he quoted me rates for a $10,000.00 whole life policy for four years, for an individual of thirty-five years of age, at less than $120.00 for the full four years. In the case of our sample, you would have added $3,000.00 worth of coverage over the entire four years, as compared to the amount of coverage the bank would offer. Through the bank the amount of coverage decreases, since the insurance company will pay out the amount still owed the bank only at the time of your death. So at the halfway point of your loan the coverage is only half the original amount. For example, using our sample car loan:

Life Insurance Through Bank	Separate Life Insurance
Amount of Coverage	Amount of Coverage
$10,610.40 (beginning)	$10,000.00 (for 48 Months)
5,305.20 (after 24 months)	Cost of Coverage $120.00
2,652.60 (after 36 months)	Savings $155.87 ($275.87 minus $120.00)
Cost of Coverage $275.87	

Not bad. Using your own insurance agent saves you a substantial sum of money and actually increases your coverage.

In fact, the savings are even greater, since the bank adds the cost of the credit life insurance policy to your loan. In this case it would mean that you would have added $104.83 in finance charges to the total loan. The net result is that the bank's credit life policy actually has a price tag of $380.70 ($275.87 + $104.83 finance charge on the $275.87, times 48 months). Your total savings in dealing with your local agent is $260.70 ($380.70 − $120.00).

This is probably one of the bank's most creative ways of stealing, since there is nothing illegal in what they are doing. I spent five years at a small bank. During that time we wrote approximately $120,000 worth of credit life insurance, of which we kept 40 percent, or $48,000. During the entire five-year period, the insurance company paid out a total of less than $5,000. Not a bad business. And this was only at one small bank. Multiply this by the total number of banks in the country, making approximate allowances for the increased volume in larger banks, and you are looking at a very large figure. The sad part of all this is that banks are playing on the fears of individuals and families who probably can ill afford any added expense to what is already an overpriced loan.

A bank cannot, by law, force you to take credit life insurance or disability insurance. The way they get around this is simply to type the policies into the loan contract and then neglect to mention the cost of the insurance when reviewing the payment schedule before you sign the note. Most loan forms are so confusing to the average person that even when the insurance is mentioned it is, at best, glossed over. You can call this what you want. I call it stealing.

Disability insurance, believe it or not, is the worse of the two. It is more expensive, mainly because the insurance company knows that the odds are, statistically, extremely slim that you will become disabled during the term of the loan. However, the odds of this happening are greater than your passing away during the same period. The net "benefit" to your family under the disability insurance will actually be less, since this type of insurance simply makes your payments only until you are back to work. Again, I worked in four different banks during my career, and in all the hundreds of thousands of premiums paid by bank customers for disability insurance, I remember only three occasions where the insurance company paid *any* monthly payments, which totaled no more than $10,000.00. Let's go back to our sample loan that shows a cost for this "service" as $413.81 and add to that cost the finance charge (for financing the total insurance premium) of $157.24, and you end up paying $571.05. With our sample loan, and with the monthly payments of $221.05, you are going to have to be disabled for almost three full months to break even—not a very good investment, especially when all you have accomplished by taking the disability insurance is to protect the bank should the worst happen. If you did become disabled the bank isn't going to repossess your car, since it is probably worth only half of what you still owe on it. They will work with you not because they are nice guys but because they don't want the problem of collecting a loan from a disabled person. This would be very bad publicity and very bad public relations. The bank would not want to sell your car, either, since they would probably take a loss by doing so.

To sum up, *never* buy credit life insurance and/or disability insurance through your bank. They are overpriced, offer less coverage than you would receive through your local insurance agent, and most of all, you are paying for insurance that benefits the bank first and your family second. Maybe the bank would be interested in paying its share of the premium?

2

MORTGAGE LENDING

Almost everyone who owns a home has borrowed money to pay for it, and almost everyone who plans to buy one faces getting a mortgage. Chances are that you were, or will be, more concerned about getting the home of your dreams than about the financial realities of a long-term mortgage. But the error of not fully understanding the financial aspects of purchasing your dream house can, over the course of your lifetime, cost you tens of thousands of dollars! The average couple views the purchase of a house simply in terms of the monthly mortgage payment and how that alone fits into the family's monthly budget. If the mortgage payments were added up, the total would probably scare you into canceling the deal. I don't have a concrete way of avoiding these unfortunate circumstances, but I can show you how to save "up front" money. And I can offer a method of saving thousands of dollars on the real cost of your home. I can't save you money on the amount you actually paid the seller, but I can show you ways to lower the amount you will pay the bank over the term of the mortgage.

First let's look at the bad news. Our mortgage example will be a $120,000.00 home for which you placed $20,000.00

down. You searched around, and the best mortgage you could secure was for $100,000.00 at 15 percent for a term of twenty-nine years. Now let's look at the actual cost of that home.

Purchase price	$120,000.00
Minus down payment	20,000.00
Mortgage	100,000.00
Monthly payments at 15%	1,266.80
Total amount repaid bank	$440,846.40

If you could take a good look at the home used in our example, would you think it is worth $440,846.40? It must be, because that's what you paid for it. There was a time that with inflation plus the tax benefit, the net result was not as damaging as it is today. Mortgage rates are high right now because most banks are afraid of the future. Historically, these rates should be roughly 2 percent above the inflation rate. But those days are gone as banks and other financial institutions are making every effort to protect their assets should inflation drive up their cost of money (the cost of acquiring deposits). Simply stated, if interest rates go up and banks have to pay the depositor higher rates, they have to charge more for the money they lend as well. Most banks are poorly managed, and their planning for the future is haphazard. They should be able to plan for various financial conditions, but they are basically lazy and would simply rather stick it to you, letting you pay for their inability to control their own destiny. There's not much we can do about this, even though mortgage rates are at present being artificially kept at a rate in excess of the norm. (Incidentally, don't expect help from the country's legislators, because the American Bankers Association is an extremely powerful lobby.)

As you can see, the ultimate cost of your home may well equal close to four times its purchase price. What can we do about it? First, let's go back to our mortgage example to see what the ultimate savings would be over the term of the mortgage if we can reduce the rate by *just ½ percent* (and here is the reason to shop for your mortgage at *every* financial institution in your area).

Monthly payments at 15%	$ 1,266.80
Total paid	440,846.40
Monthly payments at 14½%	1,227.12
Total paid	427,037.76

At first glance the savings are quite small. On a monthly basis the difference is only $39.68. Over the twenty-nine years, however, the savings amount to over $13,000.00! If you took that $39.68 every month and put it in a savings account for twenty-nine years, the $13,000.00 would more than double. You may think that's great, but you are probably wondering how you can get the bank to lower its rate by ½ percent. Here's your first chance to tell your banker a little white lie. First, you go into the bank and apply for the mortgage loan. With luck, it will be approved. Then the bank will give you the bad news that there is an additional charge for closing costs (typically 2 to 3 percent of the total borrowed), a $250 fee for appraisal of the property, and some other sundry charges that usually total an additional $500. The closing costs alone could be approximately $3,000. You're now looking at a bill for $4,000 before you even make your first mortgage payment! After doing your shopping for mortgage rates, decide on one and tell the bank to proceed with the appraisal, survey, and title search. Make sure you never pay in advance for any of these services. Simply tell your banker that you don't have your checkbook and that you'll be back in a couple of days because you have some other business that needs to be taken care of immediately. But, be sure to stress that the bank should start on the loan papers and so forth as soon as possible, because time is of the essence. The banker will not believe for a second that he can be beaten at his own game, so he will not hesitate in starting the process. By so doing, he will quickly run up a bill of approximately $1,000 that he plans to pass on to you (even though all of this work and the associated fees are for the bank's protection, not yours). Once he runs up these charges, you've got him! Be certain to call in every few days to see if the preliminary work is being completed, and as soon as it is, that is your time to revisit the bank. Explain to your banker that since your last discussion, you have had the opportunity to shop around, and you have found a much better deal. Quote him an interesst rate of ½ percent less than he is offering, and closing costs of 1 percent less. Tell him that you'd really like to do business with him, but you can't pass up the better offer. He may be mad, but he has only two choices. Either he swallows the money he has already spent on your behalf (something bankers never do), or he matches your "better" deal. Of course, you should never use the name of the "other" bank, as you don't want to give the banker a trail he can follow. Simply decline to give him any information you don't wish to divulge. If his pride won't allow him to meet your "better" offer, go to another bank and do exactly the same thing until you get what *you* want. You can afford to spend the time necessary to do this. After all, you're going to spend thousands of dollars less when you find the right bank. A word of caution: Some banks require money up front before they will do any research or preliminary work on a mortgage loan, *so stay away from them*. The good news is that there are few of these banks, and usually they are big banks in highly populated areas.

Don't forget that there are fees you have to pay the bank just for giving you the privilege of borrowing the mortgage money at an interest rate that is probably 6 percent over what it should be. First there is the title search. You shouldn't mind this too much, because you are going to need such a search, anyway. This procedure assures that you are buying a property free and clear of legal restrictions. The fee for this should run about $250. Now we get to the appraisal fee, which is approximately another $200. The appraisal is performed by the bank or someone they hire. If the bank hires someone, it usually pays him half and pockets the remainder. They're doing it again, aren't they? The appraisal fee *should not* be your expense. The information gathered through the appraisal is used by the bank to make sure there is enough equity in the home to pay off the mortgage loan should you default on the payments. Bankers like to secure themselves with collateral because it in essence releases them from the responsibility of making a prudent loan judgment. Bankers want an appraisal to guarantee their position, and on top of it all, they want *you* to pay the additional fee so they can rest easily. It's not fair, but that's the way it is. Perhaps this knowledge will help ease your conscience if you feel guilty about the need to "lie" to get what should be rightfully yours—a fair deal.

We now confront the legitimate "extortion" part of the mortgage loan, the closing costs. These represent an arbitrary fee the bank assesses for absolutely nothing. They have artificially tightened up the availability of mortgage money to justify the high cost of obtaining a mortgage, and then they want a little extra on the side. When you receive the settlement sheet at closing time, the fees (usually 2 to 3 percent of the total amount borrowed—in our example, a maximum of $3,000) will be justified as "administrative costs" and other mumbo jumbo. In reality, these charges are simply another way of jacking up the total cost to the consumer. There is absolutely no legitimate reason for these fees. The worst part about this "extortion" is that the bank misrepresents the additional fees in quoting the actual annual percentage rate (APR) at the time of closing. Since your mortgage loan is over a twenty-nine-year time span, the net effect on the APR is negligible. But what effect does this $3,000 closing cost have on the APR if you sell your house in, say, five years? Remember that our example used a mortgage rate of 15 percent. If you include the $3,000 closing cost for twenty-nine years, the APR jumps to 15.11 percent, which may be acceptable, but it is not completely fair. The banking community has figured out that the vast majority of people move, or sell their house every five years, on statistical average. If this is true (and research has substantiated that it is), what is the effect of the $3,000 closing cost on your five-year loan? *The unbelievable answer is that the closing cost adds another percent to the cost of the loan.* That 15 percent mortgage turns into 16 percent! Your bank did nothing illegal, but one can only question the integrity of a financial institution preparing documents, armed with knowledge that is not at your disposal and adding substantial expense that is not adequately explained to the buyer. If your mortgage loan runs the full twenty-nine years, the bank collects $103.45 extra per year in quasi interest ($3,000 divided by 29). However, if you sold your home in five years, the bank would collect an additional $600 per year! Hardly seems fair, does it?

The main problem with mortgages is that so much of each payment you make is applied to interest during the earlier years of the mortgage, when each payment will allow only a few dollars to be deducted from the principal. That's how a $100,000.00 mortgage turns so easily into a $440,846.40 monster. There is only one thing you can do to reduce substantially the ultimate cost of your home. We are going to do the same thing the bank does to its consumers. We are going to give them less than they bargained for. This maneuver will show you how you can turn $12,000.00 into $124,814.40, and all it's going to cost you is $50.00 a month. You see the bank does not want you ever to realize, other than casually, that payment after payment, year after year, your outstanding mortgage balance has barely decreased. But there is nothing to stop you from adding an amount over and above the monthly payment required. *When you do that, EVERY dollar over the required payment goes directly against the principal.* You might say that you can't afford an extra $50.00 a month, and my answer to that is you can't afford *not* to spend the additional $50.00. Using this payment schedule, you are going to spend a total of $600.00 per year extra on your mortgage ($50.00 per month times 12), for a total of $12,000.00, because you are going to do this for twenty years. Why twenty years? Because—and brace yourself for this—at the end of twenty years your twenty-nine-year mortgage will be paid off in full! Look at the following example (we are using our sample mortgage again, which was $100,000.00 at 15 percent for twenty-nine years):

Mortgage balance	$100,000.00
Payments	1,266.80
Total payments (29 years)	440,846.40

Mortgage balance	100,000.00	
Payments	1,316.80	($1,266.80 plus additional $50.00 principal payment)
Total payments (20 years)	316,032.00	
Net savings	124,814.40	

Here's proof positive that "a penny saved is a penny earned." Again, using our example, you can pay off your home mortgage nine years early and pocket the payments you would have made for the next nine years. Really to understand and appreciate the enormous impact of this simple approach, let's compare apples and apples. As I said, this is going to cost you an additional $600.00 per year. In return, you are going to end up saving $6,240.72 per year ($124,814.40 divided by twenty years). *This is the equivalent of an interest rate on your original investment ($600.00) of 1,040.12 percent per year!* No other legal investment activity will *ever* return this kind of dividend. And it is all so simple. Why didn't your banker give you all this information? The reason should be obvious. However, in case you missed it, the bank's job is to make money from your financial needs, and as much as it can. It doesn't care how it gets it. Ninety-nine percent of the bankers in this country are honest people, in the general sense of the word—unless you consider legal deception and misuse of general information as dishonest. If that is the case, they are far from totally honest.

Obviously, this method of saving on your mortgage is completely valid regardless of the principal, or term, or interest rate. The amount of your savings will only vary in size based on the principal amount and the amount of your additional monthly principal payment.

Some banks have a prepayment penalty (which is an amount charged you in addition to your mortgage payments) should you pay off your mortgage early. The amount of the penalty varies and cannot be stated here. They not only want the monthly payments, but they also want to tell you *how* they want the monthly payments. In today's market prepayment penalties are rare, but you have to be alert to ensure that you don't sign a mortgage agreement with this clause. A prepayment penalty can be very costly and is payable in a lump sum (usually if the mortgage loan is paid off within the first five years of its term).

THE ESCROW GAMBIT

When you open your mortgage account at a bank, the institution will more than likely demand that you open up an escrow account at the same time. These monies, collected monthly, will be set aside to pay your real-estate tax and insurance payment when due. Banks do this so they do not run into a problem if you do not pay your bills on "their" property. Often in explaining this requirement of their mortgage agreement they will gloss over this demand or tell you that it is in your best interest—i.e., you will not have to worry about your tax and insurance bill, as they will take care of it.

To set the record straight, banks require an escrow account for two reasons. One is obvious, and one is profitable—to the bank. The bank requires monthly payments in anticipation of your bills because if your house burns to the ground they want to be sure their investment is covered by insurance payable to them. Also, they don't want to find out, maybe too late, that your home is being sold for deliquent taxes. If they make the payments directly they don't have to worry about this very real possibility. Well, as fair as all this sounds, the facts are that the bank can verify the very same information, in the same timely manner, by simply requesting or requiring that you bring in your paid tax and insurance bills as they come due. Granted, this means that you will create a little more paperwork for the bank, but that's really not your problem, is it? No matter what your bank tells you about your mortgage escrow account, it is all one big lie unless they told you that they plan to make a large sum by once again using your money.

Most banks pay little or no interest on escrow accounts, and this is where their slice of the pie comes in. Keep in mind that you have already probably paid an exorbitant fee for closing costs (usually 2 to 3 percent of the total of the gross mortgage), and an appraisal fee, and the cost of a credit check, and your interest rate, and now the bank wants even more. Let me explain.

Let's use as an example a home that has a tax bill of $1,500 and an insurance bill of $300. That means you will have escrowed $1,800 during a twelve-month period, or an additional $150 per month, over and above your mortgage payment. Keeping in mind that as a rule a bank has the use of only half the monies collected by monthly payments over the span of a year, this means that you have made the bank an interest-free loan of $900 for the period of one year. Using a bank investment rate of 13 percent (bank daily investments have been as high as 22% within recent memory) means that the bank earned $117 in interest on your money. Maybe that doesn't sound too bad to you, but I don't think it's fair under the circumstances. Typically, each family will have a 30-year mortgage, and that means that the bank will earn $3,510 over the life of the mortgage—regardless.

You can see that a bank can earn a great deal of their net profits for the bank in this manner. Again, using our example, a bank with a hundred of these mortgages would earn $11,700 per year. A bank with a thousand of these mortgages would earn $117,000, and so on. Once again the bank is taking advantage of financially uneducated people and in the process taking money that is not rightfully theirs.

Actually your loss could be much larger, as in many cases banks make errors that cost homeowners thousands more. When you open your mortgage account the bank's loan officer makes an estimate of your anticipated expenses. The estimate is always high (remember, the bank wants to protect itself) and this, over a period of years, adds up. For instance: If the bank's estimate of your expenses is off by only $10 per month, this adds up to $120 per year. Therefore your escrow account, after the bills are paid, will still have a balance of $120. When this happens the bank will never on its own make you aware of this overpayment. The balance should be on your escrow statement that you receive from the bank, but who really reads or understands those statements? As you may have guessed, they are designed to meet the applicable laws as opposed to informing. So in our example, at the end of the first year the bank will have another $120 of your money to invest for their profit. At the end of ten years they will have $1,200. At the end of twenty years they will have $2,400. At 13 percent they will earn another $312, all because of their inaccuracy in estimating your escrow account. For those of you that think this is farfetched, let me tell you the news story I just heard on the local NBC-TV outlet. An elderly couple just found out that they had $9,600 in their escrow account— and have had for over ten years. Their son was looking through their mortgage papers at their request and discovered the money. It turns out that with overpayments and tax abatements of a number of years the couple had enough in their escrow account to pay off the remainder of their mortgage and still have $5,000. The sad part of all this is that the bank paid no interest on their escrow account. Using our 13 percent again, this means that this bank made $1,248 per year from these poor people. Over the ten years the bank made a total of $12,480 and in the process paid the people, whose money it really was, absolutely nothing.

Enough of this moralizing—how do we turn this built-in loss into a gain? Most of you have probably already arrived at the answer. Tell your bank no, you will not agree to open an escrow account for your mortgage. You will pay your bills by yourself and will provide them copies of the payments. Some who don't feel too comfortable being assertive may wish to tell the banker that they will open up their own escrow account at their bank, and at its option the bank may check the balance whenever it feels the need. Of course, you want to open this *interest-bearing* account in your name only, and open one that returns the most interest possible at that institution. (Remember to check not only the interest rate but also how the interest is paid—you want daily interest.) Whatever the rate of the account, it won't be as much as the bank earns on their daily investments, but even at 5.5 percent you would earn approximately $49.50 per year, or $1,485.00 over the life of a thirty-year mortgage.

If by some strange chance your bank will not go along with your wishes, you should check with the appropriate government or state agency to see if they are able, by regulation, to force you into their escrow agreement. Legally each state is different, and you may have a profitable class-action legal suit on your hands if the bank has not met its legal obligations. Of course, as I have said before, if your bank is this greedy with your money perhaps you should look for another bank.

VARIABLE-RATE MORTGAGES

Basically, variable-rate mortgage agreements change the interest rate you pay whenever the criteria under your mortgage agreement take effect. I can't tell you exactly how every variable-rate mortgage works, as the criteria that change the rate can be as different as the number of banks. If you are paying 13 percent now, and if inflation goes up, your interest rate may go to 14 percent, or if the T-bill rate escalates, your rate may go up, or any number of other facts may change the rate you pay. Banks have come up with this new gimmick for one reason only: to maintain profitability and be isolated from fluctuations in the cost of money. When you realize that banks are basically lazy and don't have the expertise to plan for the uncertainties of the future, you can see why we are now being saddled with variable-rate mortgages. The problem is that the public is being taken in by the banks' marketing package and is agreeing to variable-rate mortgages. Banks are offering the variable-rate packages at anywhere up to 3 percent below the current fixed-rate-mortgage rate, so customers are naturally taking the lower rate. Do you really think the bank is offering a variable-rate mortgage at below the fixed rate-mortgage rate if they didn't know in the long run they will make up the difference and more? Of course not.

When you take out a mortgage you have, if you're like most of us, figured your monthly income and applied it to your payments. If you're smart you've realized that there will be additional expenses each year as taxes and insurance costs escalate, but that's OK, you tell yourself, as next year you'll get a raise. All of us go through these mental gymnastics when we buy a home. At any rate, you buy the home if you can afford the mortgage, and the nice part is that as long as you choose to live there, the amount of your monthly mortage payment will never change. Assuming that all things are equal, each year your mortgage payment as a percentage of your income will drop; this is guaranteed. You can sleep at night. Now comes the variable-rate mortgage. You may very well get a raise, but the rate increase may eat up every penny of that raise and more! You have in effect put yourself in the position of having a landlord who can change your rent whenever he pleases, except in this case it may happen two or three times a year. Do rates go down more often than they go up? Of course not, and although I cannot give you every possibility, I can guarantee you that over the life of a variable-rate mortgage you will pay more than if you had taken the short-term loss of a fixed-rate mortgage. *Never* accept a variable-rate mortgage. I cannot stress this enough. I am terribly afraid that in the next ten years there will be a rash of home foreclosures that as a percentage of all homes having mortgages will rival or exceed the Depression, and it will all be because banks talked customers into variable-rate mortgages. They'll convince you that you'll save money up front; in doing so they appeal to the greed in each of us, but in the long run they will have the last laugh.

The sad part of all this is that if you anticipate a substantial drop in the mortgage rates you can always remortgage your home with another institution, as long as you do so at a lower fixed rate that will also net you enough to offset any closing fees on the new loan. The answer to all of this should therefore be simple: A variable-rate mortgage puts the bank and the economy in the driver's seat. This also holds true with mortgages that have a balloon payment. (A balloon payment is a single lump-sum payment to be paid in the future. A typical example would be a thirty-year amortized loan that runs for five years. You would make monthly payments as if you were going to for thirty years, but at the end of five years you must pay the *entire* balance still owing. This gives the bank the right to renegotiate your interest rate or force you to move your loan.) However, a fixed-rate mortgage makes you the captain of the ship. If the rates go up, you are sitting on a gold mine; if they go down, you simply move your mortgage.

All this is simply an extension of the bank's ability to convince the public that the sky is green. Any time a bank markets a new service or changes an old one you can be sure they are doing so because it makes them more money at your expense. Be terribly skeptical of such new services or changes at all times, as banks are in business to make as much money as possible. They are not, as they would have us believe, the Salvation Army.

3

NEGOTIATE YOUR LOAN RATE TO PRIME

One fact of life in the financial world is that the borrower remains at a distinct disadvantage in the lending transaction. First, the typical borrower allows himself or herself to be intimidated by the bank. You are meeting the banker on the banker's turf, which tends to lessen your confidence. The banks know this, and they make full use of the situation. If you are a first-time borrower at an institution, you can expect the following procedure: First you see the loan secretary, who will screen your preliminary loan request. Having a rough idea of your needs, she hands you the appropriate loan form to be filled out while you are waiting for the loan officer. The loan application has two purposes. Primarily it is designed to provide the bank a reasonable amount of general information. This allows a loan committee or an individual to make a decision on your request, or to pursue the matter further. The secondary purpose of the loan application is to cause you to feel uncomfortable and to make it clear to you that the bank has the upper hand. If you feel that I am exaggerating this point, let me just say that I have been part of many loan meetings where loan application forms were being designed or changed. In every case, the intended intimidation factor was a major issue. After completing the loan application you are asked to wait until the loan officer is available to interview you. It is not unusual for a customer to wait an hour or more before seeing this inquisitor. When you finally get in his office, the loan officer slowly reviews the application while you squirm in your chair. (I know of several loan officers who intentionally do this for as long as possible to unnerve the customer.) Finally the officer starts the interrogation, and from this point on you must convince the officer that you are worthy of his consideration. Generally speaking, you will not be given an answer to your loan request for a few days. You will be told that a credit check is necessary. You leave the bank with misgivings, wondering if you will be able to buy that new car. In a few days you'll receive a call with the answer. Let's assume that your loan was approved. If the loan officer did his job as instructed, he has succeeded in creating enough general intimidation that you will say absolutely nothing to rock the boat from this point forward. You're so happy to have been granted the loan that you are now willing to agree to almost anything. This is where your friendly banker really sticks it to you.

Most banks have a preset lending rate for every type of loan. Car loans are at X percent, mortgages are at another X percent, unsecured notes are at still another X percent, and so forth. This is, by far, the most unprofessional approach to lending the bank community could possibly have, and yet it is perpetuated because it is also the most profitable. What your banker hasn't told you is that loan rates are directly proportionate to the risk factor. For that reason mortgage rates have historically been lower than those for car loans, and rates for car loans have had lower rates than those for unsecured loans. In each case, the given rate is directly related to the bank's chance of losing money on the loan. An unsecured loan (without collateral) obviously has a greater possibility of loss to the bank than a mortgage loan does. Consequently, the higher risk factor is reflected in the higher interest rate.

But the bank never applies this doctrine to you as an individual. For example, if your credit rating is exemplary, why then is your past performance not reflected in a lower rate for an individual loan request? Should a customer with an excellent credit rating and 40 percent down on a new car pay the same rate of interest as a person with a marginal credit rating and a 5 percent down payment? Whatever our common sense dictates should be the answer to this question, the fact is that most banks in most lending situations do not vary an interest rate on an individual basis.

Bankers justify this by balancing their entire loan portfolio on "good," "marginal," or "poor risk" bases. It is an accepted fact among bankers that a predetermined portion of any given loan category will go bad and create a loss. The existing philosophy is that losses can be offset by creating a single-rate approach to each type of loan. With the safe loans the risk factor was negligible to begin with. The rates on these safe loans are inflated to defray the losses on riskier loans. Your credit rating, assuming it is good, should not simply allow you to acquire financing. It should also provide you with a rate decrease based on the *individual* factor of risk that *your* loan represents to the bank.

The banks' overall cost of money will give them a base-line minimum on any given loan, but beyond that there should be a judgment allowance by the loan officer for the most desirable loans. From your standpoint you must begin to take the attitude with your bank that your business is important, and you expect certain consideration based on your excellent loan record. Don't lose sight of the fact, too, that your existing account relationships are also profitable to the bank.

Banks often cite the *prime rate* as an excuse for charging you interest rates that often come close to those of a loan shark. As a customer, you should be aware that the prime rate is *the rate that banks charge their best commercial customers for borrowing.* Your bank may go on to tell you that if it is charging General Motors X percent, certainly you can understand why you are being charged X percent plus. This logic, of course, is ill-founded to begin with and certainly questionable in these times of commercial bankruptcies, which are at an all-time high. You and other customers like you are the real "bread and butter" business to banks. However, you continue to be ignored in terms of rate considerations because you aren't equipped with sufficient general banking knowledge to refute such illogical arguments. Most customers simply ask what the rate is for a specific type of loan and blindly accept it without question. This is most unfortunate, because *interest rates are negotiable,* and here lies the main point of this chapter. When confronted with this from your banker you *must* tell him that as you see it banks loan money to companies and individuals and there are good and bad loans in each category. With your payment record you *are* the General Motors of the latter. The only difference between you and GM is that your loan request is smaller.

First make an objective appraisal of both the desirability of your continuing relationship with the bank and the desirability of your loan request. If you are an average customer with an average credit rating, accept the quoted rate and be happy that you were able to arrange the financing you wanted. If you are a good bank customer with a quality credit rating, then it is time to roll up your sleeves and do something to reduce the quoted loan rate. To accomplish this, you must first realize, and then convince the loan officer, that you are worthy of a rate reduction to the prime rate or better. Okay, so you're not rich—*but you pay your bills on time.* That's more than a lot of commercial customers can boast, and yet these businesses often borrow at the prime rate with little or no collateral. The point here is, regardless of your apprehension (initially planned by your bank), *you must insist on a better rate on every loan request.* If you consistently take this approach, you will succeed in convincing your banker that you are someone to be reckoned with, and you will save yourself thousands of dollars throughout your lifetime. A 1 percent reduction on an $8,500.00 loan for forty-eight months results in a saving of $340.00 over the course of the loan. On a $75,000.00 mortgage for twenty-nine years, the savings at only a 1 percent reduction amounts to $20,660.76 over the life of the mortgage. The saddest part of the rate game is that people seldom capture the opportunity to negotiate their position. The result is that you are unknowingly assisting the bank in taking advantage of you.

Rates are negotiable, but only if you pursue the negotiation. This may very well mean that you will have to skip over the loan officer and go straignt to the president. If you're *still* not successful, you may have to go straight to the board of directors. The more informed you are about the total structure of the bank, and the more adamant you are about not being placed into a loan category that is beneath your credit rating, the better your chances are of receiving fair treatment. Bankers don't like to have outside pressure put on them. They are accustomed to having the advantage on the customer. They will usually retreat the moment your voice gets louder, or the moment you tell them that you want to see Mr. Higher Up. Of course, this demand on your part for prime-rate borrowing consideration will be much more successful in a smaller institution because the big banks simply don't much care what you think. Big banks will tell you to take your business elsewhere if you won't play by their rules. Smaller banks, on the other hand, need your business. To prove my point, here are some comparisons.

Let's compare your position in a bank with assets of $20 million as opposed to a bank with assets of $20 billion. A $9,000 car loan from a $20 million bank is the equivalent of a $9 million loan from a $20 billion bank. Are you beginning to see why you *must* do business at a small bank? A $75,000 mortgage from a $20 million bank is the equivalent of a $75 million loan from a $20 billion bank. In other words, you *are* one of your bank's best "commercial customers" if you choose the right bank. If this is true, it should be clear that you have every right to expect, and if necessary demand, your bank's best loan considerations. The savings to you can be immense.

With installment loans (monthly payment loans), many people get so involved with the monthly obligations that they fail to take into consideration the bottom-line total expense to them. Almost every loan customer I ever worked with would buy the bank's total loan package, including the loan rate, as long as the monthly payments fit into the family's budget. Although this is a consideration that must not be ignored, it should be one of the least important considerations in the art of loan negotiation. Look at the bottom line and settle for nothing less than the consideration your loan request deserves. Often all it takes is for a customer to ask, and the rate is lowered. The problem is that not enough people ask, which leads the bank to become less responsive to the needs of the consumer while reinforcing the bank's arrogance. From the examples presented here, you can see that maybe you're unimportant to the big bank, but you are a *big shot* to a smaller institution. You will succeed in reminding your banker, through intelligent financial rate negotiation, that you expect to be treated like a big shot. And you'll save a lot of money in the process.

4

PARTICIPATION LOANS: LOANS ABOVE THE BANK'S LEGAL LENDING LIMIT

Since I have consistently and strongly recommended that you deal esclusively with a smaller bank, I must tell you that there are some negatives in doing so. One major drawback is that a smaller bank may not be able to service your loan request due to a legally imposed "lending limit." Simply stated, a national bank may not lend to one individual, or group of people with a like interest, an amount in excess of 10 percent of the bank's capital, surplus, undivided profits, and reserves. In a $20 million bank this would mean that they cannot lend you more than $110,000, for example. With the cost of homes today and the potential needs of a small business, your immediate lending source may be of no value to your needs.

Most smaller banks simply turn down out-of-hand loan requests in excess of their lending limit. They don't want to be bothered, and they don't intend to "risk" a substantial loan loss. When faced with this possibility, the banker will usually apologize and explain that the loan is over the bank's legal lending limit.

Since having an immediate lending source is so important,

doing business at a smaller bank may hamper your plans—something you should try to avoid. Fortunately, there is a solution to this problem. Your banker is aware of this but doesn't want to be bothered with it unless absolutely necessary. The logical recourse is a participation loan. Your small bank will do all the paperwork and carry your loan on its books but will sell to another bank the portion that is over its legal lending limit. Let's say you make a loan request for $125,000 to a small bank that has a lending limit of $95,000. The bank must sell at least $30,000 to another financial institution. You may be wondering why a bank would not follow this practice on a fairly consistent basis. Bankers would just as soon not be bothered, since a participation loan involves a great deal of extra work, both in loan preparation and monthly servicing. But that's the banker's problem. Yours is to secure the loan.

Assuming that you have a valid loan request and are a good customer of the bank, just having the knowledge of a participation loan can place the banker in a position where he cannot easily refuse your request. The strategy here is to let him dig a hole for himself. If you ever receive a loan turndown because the application is over the bank's lending limit, question the banker as to the merits of the loan, disregarding the overloan situation. Ask for the banker's help in reviewing the merits of the loan itself. Then ask if the bank would make the loan if it were below its lending limit. Bankers always fall for this line and nine times out of ten will answer in the affirmative even when they wouldn't touch the loan with a ten-foot pole. Once a banker has an easy out (in this case the overloan situation), he will agree to almost anything. Your banker will proceed to tell you how much he would like to help you if it weren't for the darn law about lending limits. You're such a good customer, and the loan request is solid. Of course, the bank would help if only it could. It is now time to ask for a small favor from your friendly, helpful banker.

Tell the banker that since all your accounts are at that bank, you will have to apply at another institution that really doesn't know you, and your request will be at a distinct disadvantage there. Ask your banker to write a general "To Whom

It May Concern" letter explaining that his or her bank would have made the loan except that it was over their legal lending limit. Also suggest that the banker include anything else that would indicate to another financial institution that you are a good credit risk. I have never seen a banker refuse a request of this nature. The banker knows the letter doesn't obligate him to anything, it keeps you happy, and it succeeds in getting you off his back. When you get your letter, thank him profusely, and you are on your merry way. Little does he know that he hasn't seen the last of you and your loan request.

The next step is to wait a few days, to eliminate an appearance of preplanning on your part. If the bank officer who wrote the letter was not the president, visit him. If the president wrote the letter, then visit one of the bank's directors. In either case, produce the letter and tell the person that you were out shopping for the loan at different financial institutions. Explain that two other banks indicated they didn't believe the statements made in the letter because if you were such a good customer your own bank would certainly have processed your loan and sold the overloan amount to a participating institution. In a similar situation, they would have gone to a correspondent bank they do business with. Tell him that you now have a limited understanding of a participation loan, and you would like to know why the original officer you spoke with didn't offer you that service instead of turning you down. On top of that, you now feel most embarrassed because you were made to look foolish at two other local financial institutions. Appear to be extremely upset and perplexed. First they turned you down, and now because of the officer's letter, you seriously doubt if you can ever get a loan at the other institutions. Under no circumstance should you reveal the names of the mythical institutions, because he can easily check with someone there. If you are questioned, just say you'd rather not go into that because enough personal damage has already been done.

You have now neatly placed the ball in this person's court. Bluntly ask what he or she is going to do to correct the situation. Stress that this has always been your bank and you do all your business here. You have been caused a great deal of personal embarrassment as well as being turned down in a loan request when it appears that your bank could have served you in the first place. I have seen this ploy work effectively a number of times with different variations. As a matter of fact, I have yet to see it fail. The banker sees no easy way out, what with the written letter and your "new" knowledge of participation loans. The banker will have no choice but to make a few allowances and concessions that the bank should have made in the first place and will be willing to accommodate you now because the bank doesn't like to be caught in a lie. Further, the banker can't afford for you to tell your friends, family, and God knows who else that you were treated in such an unprofessional manner. Unless the banker delivers at this point, he or she is admitting by inaction that the officer who turned you down originally was lying, or the staff is unskilled in not being aware of the ability to make overloans.

This ruse will work with many different banking problems, or anywhere else, for that matter. Its effectiveness depends on the banker's reluctance to do his or her job efficiently. The banker will take the easy way out whenever possible. If that takes the form of an actual lie, or an unspoken lie, it really doesn't matter. As long as they can get rid of you in the shortest amount of time, and maybe keep you happy in the process, then all is well. It is unfortunate that a bank customer must use a ploy to receive the service he or she deserves, but often it is the only way. Again, we are not trying to change any rules. We're simply learning to work around them and achieve the desired results.

5

MAKE THE BEST
OF A BAD SITUATION

At one time or another you may have a financial problem that causes a loan to become delinquent. The average person, when confronted with this uncomfortable situation, tries to avoid the inevitable phone call from the bank. To compound the problem, when the bank does call, the customer makes excuses and tries to buy time hoping that something will work out. This course of action is a blueprint for disaster. All that really was accomplished was to alert the bank that your loan has become a problem. After several of these phone calls it is highly probable that you will find yourself without a car. You may even be privileged with a visit from your banker, which is an embarrassment to you and your family. There *is* a better solution when your loan agreements can't be met.

The first thing you *must* do is never allow a loan payment to be past due *under any circumstances*. This doesn't mean that you can always make the payment on time. It simply means *never let it become past due*. You accomplish this sleight of hand by personally contacting your bank *before the due date* of your loan payment. You explain the circumstances surrounding your problem while at the same time explaining that you are very concerned about your credit rating with the bank. Explain that you expect to resume regular payments in three months (or whatever time period is comfortable for you), and ask for a loan extension. The banker will jump at this chance for a number of reasons. First, you have shown good faith in revealing that there are extenuating circumstances regarding your financial situation. Second, it will save the banker a great deal of time and trouble if you come to him or her without the banker having to chase you down. Last, by giving you an extension of time, the bank makes a few extra dollars. This procedure will prevent your name from appearing on the bank's delinquent loan report to the board of directors and examiners. You have done the loan officer a big favor, and in so doing you have bought, for example, three additional months of much-needed time. At the end of your extension you will be in a position to take advantage of what was a losing proposition before the extension. Assume now that you have tried to get things back on track with your payments but are still having problems. Now it is time to revisit your bank and play the second card in your hand. Once the loan officer gave you the extension (an option most consumers are not aware of), he or she inadvertently became a party to your unfortunate predicament. The banker now is faced with explaining to the board and examiners why you were granted an extension, since now you are on the delinquency report and would have been months ago without the loan officer's assistance—that is, unless he is of further assistance. *Ask for another extension.* Most loan officers would balk at this second request. However, some would be so afraid of losing the loan that they will be agreeable. If not, then it's time to explain that you could make your loan payments on time if your total monthly expenditures were not as high as they presently are. If you weren't saddled with seven (or whatever number) separate payments each month, you could definitely meet your obligations. If your banker doesn't pick up on this immediately (which he probably will), ask him if the bank could consolidate your additional loans along with your present loan to create a single payment. Emphatically stress that this is the only way you can get to square one financially. This type of loan is called a consolidation loan.

Banks seldom make such loans (they are not in business to help anyone except themselves) unless they are bailing themselves out of the hole, too. From an economical point of view, I don't recommend consolidation loans, because you are refinancing already financed money. This gets awfully expensive. Yet when faced with a financial crisis, it may be the only alternative.

If all else fails, casually mention that you may have no other choice but to file bankruptcy, even though you don't want to. At this point your banker will certainly sit up and take notice! In a bankruptcy the bank stands to lose the entire loan, or at least a portion if there is collateral involved. In a Chapter 13 bankruptcy, a bank often is made to wait an inordinately long time even to receive a small portion of what it is due. It is therefore in the bank's best interest to play ball with a customer who is having difficulty, rather than to push him or her into filing for bankruptcy. Yet, unless you can trap the bank into a further commitment on your behalf, the chances of receiving cooperation are slim. *You must go to the banker first,* set his or her mind at ease, and get the banker in deeper than under normal circumstances. I have seen case after case of customers coming out ahead by holding the carrot in front of a loan officer who is more concerned with trying to cover his tail. You must do to the bank what it did to you when you first applied for the loan. You wanted something the bank had (money), and you were put through the wringer to get it. Now you have something the bank wants (your payment), and your banker may just have to make some gigantic concessions to assist you in meeting your obligation.

Of course, I'm not suggesting that anyone reading this should intentionally be unresponsive to meeting his or her obligations. Unfortunately, bank officers have a very real tendency to lump all past-due loans into a general category of "deadbeat," and consequently you are treated as such. The banker who was so nice when you opened up your new checking account, or applied for that new-car loan, will ruthlessly rip out your heart if you hit the past-due list. Bankers will do whatever they feel is necessary to protect themselves in the eyes of their employer. They really don't care about the bank, because in most cases the bank has a sufficient loan loss reserve to more than cover the anticipated yearly loss on loans. What the banker *really* cares about is keeping his job. Making bad loans, or not collecting outstanding loans, is simply not conducive to career advancement. Because of the necessity to protect himself or herself, the banker breaks the law, either because the banker is ignorant of the law or hopes the customer is. This brings us to our next subject: overly aggressive collection techniques.

Banks are highly regulated, but unfortunately, the regulations are very seldom enforced, especially state laws concerning collection techniques. Bank officers know this—and they know how to take advantage of it. Rest assured, however, that there are laws that outline what is permissible in a collection matter. If the consumer will investigate his or her rights, the rewards can be astounding.

Once your bank (and this applies to any company extending credit, as well as a collection agency) starts putting on the pressure for a payment, *immediately start keeping a diary of all communications* initiated by the bank in its effort to collect your loan. If possible, have a family member or friend present during these communications. You may need a witness to prove your point. If an extension phone is available, have your friend listen to the conversation. The point here is that once it becomes apparent that a true adversary relationship exists between you and the bank, you want to have a complete and true record if you go to court. Often a loan officer will stray so far out of legal bounds that your record (when presented to the bank's president and legal counsel) will force the bank to suggest a bargain with you.

Make careful note of any threatening comments, even if you just *feel* threatened. Actual threats are another matter entirely. If the bank threatens to repossess your car, for example, and then does not do so, you have a very good case for harassment. Phone calls at odd hours, or to your place of business are, in most cases, not considered appropriate. A threat to destroy your credit rating is stepping over the line. If the bank attempts to talk with your children, or discusses your financing with your friends or neighbors, this is definitely worth writing down for future reference. There are as many different techniques as there are loan collectors, and I have not met one who doesn't occasionally step over the line of propriety on a fairly consistent basis. Banks get away with it because you become intimidated or indifferent. You should pay your obligations willingly, but when you absolutely cannot, based on a legitimate reason, you are entitled by law to certain considerations.

If the bank reposses your car, don't automatically assume that they have the right to do so. Sometimes the bank officer will come to your home and state that he or she is there to reposssess your car. The officer then produces the title to the car and tells you that you must sign the title as seller. Nine times out of ten the customer does exactly what he or she is told, not knowing that he or she is under no obligation at this point. But once you have signed, the bank will claim that you willingly gave them the collateral. If the bank repossesses any collateral without your knowledge, report it stolen immediately. Most repossessions are not accompanied with proper legal documentation, nor does the bank officer notify the local police in every case. Justice would certainly be served if the bank officer had to explain to the local police chief why he was driving a car that didn't legally belong to him. The point here is: Don't do anything the bank officer suggests without first consulting your lawyer.

6

PREPARING YOUR FINANCIAL STATEMENT

When you need to borrow, you are going to be asked to prepare a personal financial statement. This will be mandatory when you borrow on an unsecured basis. How you prepare this statement will, quite possibly, make the difference between success and failure in your loan request.

Some loan officers will offer to assist you in preparing this statement. If this happens, politely decline. Take the statement home and prepare it at your leisure. The loan officer may appear to be helping, but he or she has ulterior motives. The officer wants to make sure you don't inflate your current financial position. But you need to do just that if you are going to secure the loan you want.

Rule number one: *Never lie* on a personal financial statement. To do so in an effort to secure a loan is against the law. And although most infractions of this nature go unpunished by themselves, encouraging a bank officer to make a poor financial judgment based on erroneous information will most assuredly wind up in court or in front of a grand jury—an interesting paradox. Dishonest bank employees (guilty of theft, embezzlement, or a defalcation) are presented the opportunity to resign (to save the bank public embarrassment);

"dishonest" customers go to jail. My point here is not to condemn the moral ineptness of banks but rather to show you how to inflate a personal financial statement legitimately without going to jail.

Obviously, all items on a personal statement that can be verified must be presented properly. Referring to our example, you can see that items such as nonmarketable securities on the asset side of the ledger must not be tampered with, because if you include a figure that is nonexistent, the bank can prove that this was an outright fabrication. On the liability side, you cannot alter the amount of your mortgage obligation, since this can also be easily verified. Please review Forms 1 and 2 to see how you can look substantially more affluent than you really are.

Clearly, the first form presents a different picture from the second, but we did not lie to the bank. The items that can be easily verified were reported accurately. Those that were open to subjective interpretation we reported on the high side. Let's examine the items open to debate:

1. Cash on hand and in banks: We increased this by $2,000, because it can always be said that we had money at home or in our safe-deposit box. There is no way this can be *proven* to be wrong.

2. Real estate owned: We increased this by $25,000, since this is *our* opinion regarding the market value of our home. If questioned, we could say that it was our understanding that homes in the area were selling in this price range.

3. Automobiles and personal property: They have asked for your opinion of *all* additional assets. This is, to some degree, subjective opinion.

4. Other assets: Again, it is our *reasonable* opinion that the boat and construction tools are worth the reported amounts. we may be wrong, but as long as we haven't stretched the truth too far, we're on safe ground here.

5. Sources of income: I included this in the examples because it gives you an opportunity to provide the bank with an added feeling of security. This may not be specif-

ically applicable to your situation, but if your company has a bonus plan, you can inflate (within reason) as long as it is stated that this is an "anticipated" salary increase at year end. You can't just make something like this up, but if there is even a remote possibility of additional funds, report them.

Simply by taking advantage of the obvious weaknesses in the personal financial statement and using astute subjectivity, you can become a more desirable loan customer with just a few aditional strokes of your pen. In this case we have increased our net worth by $45,000, or 116.96 percent. The amount for sources of income has been increased by $7,000 or 29.16 percent. Let's say you were applying for an unsecured loan of $8,000 for thirty-six months. What do the changes in our example statements do to the ratios the loan officer may be concerned with?

Borrowing to net worth:	Form 1 = 20.56% Form 2 = 9.47%
Repayment percent of total income for 36 months:	Form 1 = 11.11% Form 2 = 8.6%

In each case, the lower the percentage, the more desirable the loan. There are other considerations, to be sure. But you can see that you would stand a much better chance of making the loan officer happier with Form 2 than with Form 1. Even after the officer discounts a percentage of your statement (which he will do in either case), your percentage of improvement will remain the same. If you are borrowing on an unsecured basis you will always need to prepare a personal financial statement. But I recommend that you prepare one for your banker in any case, because you can impress him or her with your inflated figures and your obvious financial knowledge.

Many people prepare financial statements when they are not necessary, or even requested by the bank. They are then offered to the loan officer without a signature. More often

PERSONAL FINANCIAL STATEMENT

IMPORTANT: Read these directions before completing this Statement.

☒ If you are applying for individual credit in your own name and are relying on your own income or assets and not the income or assets of another person as the basis for repayment of the credit requested complete only Sections 1 and 3

☐ If you are applying for joint credit with another person complete all Sections providing information in Section 2 about the joint applicant

☐ If you are applying for individual credit but are relying on income from alimony child support or separate maintenance or on the income or assets of another person as a base for repayment of the credit requested complete all Sections providing information in Section 2 about the person whose alimony support or maintenance payments or income or assets you are relying

☐ If the statement relates to your guaranty of the indebtedness of other person(s) firm(s) or corporation(s) complete Sections 1 and 3

TO:

SECTION 1 - INDIVIDUAL INFORMATION (Type or Print)	SECTION 2 - OTHER PARTY INFORMATION (Type or Print)
Name **John Smith**	Name
Residence Address **115 Jones St.**	Residence Address
City State & Zip **Anywhere, USA**	City State & Zip
Position or Occupation **Foreman**	Position or Occupation
Business Name **Jackson Construction**	Business Name
Business Address **222 Thomas St.**	Business Address
City State & Zip **Anywhere, USA**	City State & Zip
Res Phone **555-2232** Bus Phone **555-5767**	Res Phone Bus Phone

SECTION 3 - STATEMENT OF FINANCIAL CONDITION AS OF __1/31__ 19 _84_

ASSETS (Do not include Assets of doubtful value)	In Dollars (Omit cents)		LIABILITIES	In Dollars (Omit cents)	
Cash on hand and in banks		500	Notes payable to banks secured	4	500
U S Gov t & Marketable Securities see Schedule A		-0-	Notes payable to banks unsecured		-0-
Non Marketable Securities See Schedule B		500	Due to brokers		-0-
Securities held by broker in margin accounts	2	000	Amounts payable to others secured		-0-
Restricted or control stocks		-0-	Amounts payable to others unsecured		-0-
Partial interest in Real Estate Equities			Accounts and bills due		-0-
see Schedule C		-0-	Unpaid income tax		-0-
Real Estate Owned see Schedule D	50	000	Other unpaid taxes and interest		-0-
Loans Receivable		500	Real estate mortgages payable		
Automobiles and other personal property	13	000	see Schedule D	27	500
Cash value life insurance-see Schedule E		900	Other debts itemize		-0-
Other assets itemize					
Boat	2	500			
Construction Tools	1	000			
			TOTAL LIABILITIES	32	000
			NET WORTH	38	900
TOTAL ASSETS	70	900	TOTAL LIAB. AND NET WORTH	70	900

SOURCES OF INCOME FOR YEAR ENDED **Current** 19___	PERSONAL INFORMATION
Salary, bonuses & commissions $ **24,000.00**	Do you have a will? **NO** if so name of executor
Dividends	
Real estate income	Are you a partner or officer in any other venture? If so describe
Other income (Alimony, child support, or separate maintenance)	**No**
Income need not be revealed if you do not wish to have it	Are you obligated to pay alimony child support or separate maintenance payments? If so describe
considered as a basis for repaying this obligation)	**No**
	Are any assets pledged other than as described on schedules? If so describe
TOTAL $ **24,000.00**	**No**
CONTINGENT LIABILITIES	Income tax settled through (date) **Current**
Do you have any contingent liabilities? If so describe	Are you a defendant in any suits or legal actions?
None	**No**
As indorser co maker or guarantor? $	Personal bank accounts carried at
On leases or contracts? $	**First National Bank**
Legal claims $	
Other special debt $	Have you ever been declared bankrupt? If so describe
Amount of contested income tax liens $	**No**

(COMPLETE SCHEDULES AND SIGN ON REVERSE SIDE)

PERSONAL FINANCIAL STATEMENT

IMPORTANT: Read these directions before completing this Statement.

☒ If you are applying for individual credit in your own name and are relying on your own income or assets and not the income or assets of another person as the basis for repayment of the credit requested complete only Sections 1 and 3

☐ If you are applying for joint credit with another person complete all Sections providing information in Section 2 about the joint applicant

☐ If you are applying for individual credit but are relying on income from alimony, child support or separate maintenance or on the income or assets of another person as a basis for repayment of the credit requested complete all Sections providing information in Section 2 about the person whose alimony support or maintenance payments or income or assets you are relying on

☐ If this statement relates to your guaranty of the indebtedness of other person(s) firm(s) or corporation(s) complete Sections 1 and 3

TO:

SECTION 1 - INDIVIDUAL INFORMATION (Type or Print)	SECTION 2 - OTHER PARTY INFORMATION (Type or Print)
Name **John Smith**	Name
Residence Address **115 Jones St.**	Residence Address
City State & Zip **Anywhere, USA**	City State & Zip
Position or Occupation **Foreman**	Position or Occupation
Business Name **Jackson Construction**	Business Name
Business Address **222 Thomas St.**	Business Address
City State & Zip **Anywhere, USA**	City State & Zip
Res Phone **555-2232** Bus Phone **555-5767**	Res Phone Bus Phone

SECTION 3 - STATEMENT OF FINANCIAL CONDITION AS OF ___1/31___ 19 _84_

ASSETS (Do not include Assets of doubtful value)	In Dollars (Omit cents)		LIABILITIES	In Dollars (Omit cents)	
Cash on hand and in banks	2	500	Notes payable to banks secured	4	500
U S Gov t & Marketable Securities see Schedule A		-0-	Notes payable to banks unsecured		-0-
Non-Marketable Securities See Schedule B		500	Due to brokers		-0-
Securities held by broker in margin accounts	2	000	Amounts payable to others secured		-0-
Restricted or control stocks		-0-	Amounts payable to others unsecured		-0-
Partial interest in Real Estate Equities see Schedule C		-0-	Accounts and bills due		-0-
			Unpaid income tax		-0-
Real Estate Owned see Schedule D	75	000	Other unpaid taxes and interest		-0-
Loans Receivable		500	Real estate mortgages payable see Schedule D	27	500
Automobiles and other personal property	27	500			
Cash value life insurance-see Schedule E		900	Other debts itemize		
Other assets itemize					
Boat	5	000			
Construction Tools	2	500			
			TOTAL LIABILITIES	32	000
			NET WORTH	84	400
TOTAL ASSETS	116	400	TOTAL LIAB AND NET WORTH	116	400

SOURCES OF INCOME FOR YEAR ENDED **Current** 19___	PERSONAL INFORMATION
Salary bonuses & commissions $ **24,000.00**	Do you have a will? **No** if so name of executor
Dividends	
Real estate income	Are you a partner or officer in any other venture? If so describe **No**
Other income (Alimony, child support, or separate maintenance income need not be revealed if you do not wish to have it considered as a basis for repaying this obligation)	Are you obligated to pay alimony, child support or separate maintenance payments? If so describe **No**
Anticipated Bonus **7,000.00**	Are any assets pledged other than as described on schedules? If so describe **No**
TOTAL $ **31,000.00**	
CONTINGENT LIABILITIES	Income tax settled through (date) **Current**
Do you have any contingent liabilities? If so describe	Are you a defendant in any suits or legal actions? **No**
None	
As indorser co maker or guarantor? $	Personal bank accounts carried at
On leases or contracts? $	**First National Bank**
Legal claims $	
Other special debt $	Have you ever declared bankrupt? If so describe **No**
Amount of contested income tax liens $	

(COMPLETE SCHEDULES AND SIGN ON REVERSE SIDE)

than not, the officer will not notice the missing signature, since he didn't request the financial statement in the first place. When the time comes for a required statement, you can simply say that the bank already has one on file. What the loan officer may overlook is that it still remains unsigned. The best strategy here is to prepare the statement well in advance of a need and have a family member drop it off at the bank for you. You can accomplish the same results by mailing the statement before it is needed. The importance of this is that an unsigned financial statement is absolutely worthless if the bank decides to pursue the matter in court. In fact, the bank will, in all likelihood, not bring up the subject in court, since this tends to show that it was remiss in showing reasonable care in accepting and processing the financial statement.

It is unfortunate that inflating a personal financial statement is necessary. An individual should be able to tell the whole truth, and receive a fair and equitable loan decision from a bank. Experience, however, shows that this is not always the case. Loan officers are generally afraid to make a mistake. One big loan decision mistake, or several small ones, can lead to dismissal and in some cases even the end of a banking career. It then becomes your job to create an image the loan officer can live with, even if the image is not totally realistic. This can be accomplished by creative financial statement preparation. Banks, expecially smaller ones, tend to believe that they are dealing with a financially uneducated populace and therefore are subject to believing that financial statements prepared by individuals are not inflated. The banks then base their decision accordingly. You must take advantage of this flaw.

7

THE CREDIT DECISION

Understanding how the bank arrives at its answer to your loan request is essential to successful and intelligent borrowing. During your initial conversation with your banker, the answers you provide to the questions will contribute much regarding the bank's decision on your loan. During the first interview all the information your banker feels he or she needs will not be available. Therefore it must be obtained through other means. First let's review the Five C's of Credit, what they are, how they are applied, and how they *should* be applied.

CHARACTER

This is the most important of the Five C's. A person of unquestionable character can often receive a "yes" to a loan request that might otherwise have been turned down. Assessment of character is most often arrived at by checking the credit rating of the borrower. Your past payment record, especially with the bank you are dealing with, is the critical criterion here.

CAPACITY

This is the management ability factor, determining how well you manage your affairs. Further, it is a quantitative measurement of how successful you have been in the past in regard to your personal finances and your career. Successful people receive a high score; others do not.

CAPITAL

This is the amount of money you have at any given time. It indicates to the bank that you have enough assets to repay the loan. It is a measure of financial stability that indicates you have earned the right to borrow money.

COLLATERAL

Collateral is the bank's extra protection. It cannot make a bad loan good, but it can make a good loan even better. If you have a weakness in one of the other areas of lending criteria, sufficient collateral may swing the banker's decision in your favor. However, collateral alone will not be enough for a banker to grant your loan request.

CONDITIONS

Most consumer loans do not take into primary consideration the conditions factor. This is generally reserved for business loans. It would, for example, be a poor bank investment to lend money to a new business during a depression. The economic conditions surrounding the loan request, in other words, may have some effect. Conditions play a lesser part in personal loan requests, to the extent that they affect the lender's frame of mind. When times are tough economically, the banker doesn't care about anything but the conditions. Witness the financial community's reaction toward mortgage lending during the past few years. The conditions adversely affected practically every loan request for a residential mortgage.

When applied fairly, the Five C's of Credit are equitable both to the banker and the consumer. Unfortunately, the Five C's of Credit, although they should still all be adhered to by bankers, have been reduced to the Three C's of Credit: capital, collateral, and conditions.

As I have said before, banks are profit centers, not service centers. Banks are insensitive to the specific needs of individuals. They service just enough consumers to meet the minimum requirements of the law. When these token adherences to the law are met, banks turn completely to their investment portfolio to satisfy their desire for a high net return. This practice is responsible for cutting the Five C's of Credit down to three. Essentially this scaling down secures the bank from possible losses and at the same time eliminates the work of dealing with numerous small loans. This can be substantiated by reading any bank's financial report. There was a time when a bank's main lending needs coincided with the consumer's borrowing needs, and this was reflected in the high percentage of individual loans. Today the personal loan in any given bank is far overshadowed by the big-borrower loan. Banks can no longer claim, with any degree of validity, to be of service to anyone but themselves.

Let's review the new Three C's of Credit.

CAPITAL

Stripping away the tinsel, the capital criterion simply means that if you have $100, the bank is more than willing to loan you $50 *if* the $100 is deposited at that bank! I know bankers who joke about the guy who needs to borrow a small amount of money. At the same time, the loan department officers are out spending a bundle on lunches, trying to convince a big company that it should expand corporate operations and in the process borrow huge sums of money from the bank. That's exactly what the bank wants. They want to lend money—large sums to corporations that don't really need it.

This is the safest loan possible. Remember that a bank must, by its charter, serve an examiner-acceptable percentage of the general public, and it is your job to be among the customers they are willing to serve. It is important not to appear too anxious in your loan request. That is why you should stop in before you really need the money and casually talk things over, telling the banker that you may pay cash for that new car, but just in case you decide not to liquidate some of your investments, you're interested in discussing a loan. If you're planning to buy a Ford, tell him that you're going to buy a Buick. Later you can tell him you changed your mind because you just don't like the current models. Make up whatever story you want, but *present the image that you really don't need the loan.* This is another reason that you need to inflate your personal financial statement.

COLLATERAL

Collateral should have no bearing whatsoever on the loan decision. This is a strong statement, but I have reasons for making it. The loan decision should be made solely on the merits of the individual and the particular loan request. Any good loan officer (of which there are very few) would agree. However, banks as a whole want to own the goods (collateral), and through the loan agreement they want to lend the goods to you. Banks feel secure in knowing they can always repossess collateral. Money is another thing completely. Actually, collateral should simply decrease the bank's loan risk and thereby reduce the loan rate you are being charged. But collateral simply gets you the loan, and does nothing to reduce your interest expense. Home mortgages are a good example. Typically, the bank wants at least 30 percent down before you can obtain a loan. Considering the current cost of housing, that would mean that the bank has $25,000 to $30,000 of your money, as well as the first lien on the property involved. In addition, the property is an appreciating asset. Consequently and conveniently, the bank's position generally improves with each passing year. Additionally, a bank wants 15 percent interest and 3 percent closing costs. Historically, home mortgages were reasonable in terms of interest rates, because they were the safest loan a bank could make. Over the years bankers became dissatisfied with that position, because the loans didn't return the kind of high rates needed. So the financial community artificially created a tight mortgage money situation until you were convinced that you should be happy to pay today's exorbitant rates.

Collateral and its necessity (in the banker's mind) is another reason you must convince the bank, through legal deception, that you are a cut above the norm and are deserving of special consideration. If you accomplish this, as outlined in previous chapters, your banker will have to cut the loan interest rate when receiving collateral from you. Simply stated, if you convince the banker that you are deserving of a loan on your personal merits alone, your collateral "card" can be played for an interest-rate reduction. If not, your collateral will simply get you the loan—nothing more.

CONDITIONS

The lending criterion of establishing *your* worth as opposed to the worth of your collateral applies today, because we are now learning how tough the economy can be. The situation isn't as bad as it was fifty years ago, but the old rules just don't apply to banks and bankers today. The rule today seems to be that when things get tough, good banks make more money than ever, and bad banks curl up and die. This gives the wise consumer two excellent lending opportunities. The average guy is out of luck, since the bank will block his money supply immediately. Those who have successfully tempted their banker are now in the position of making hay in the middle of the night, so to speak. The bank in financial straits will curtail all lending, and only those with impeccable credit ratings will be able to acquire credit. Healthy banks will always have available funds for those individuals with good ratings. However, with these banks your borrowing worth may have doubled in hard times if you are willing to pay the added interest charge. You have to understand that banks, even in difficult times, have a problem with monthly paydowns (the amount of loans paid back during a given month). Even though a bank may not want to make additional new loans, it has to replace the monthly paydowns to remain profitable. Your desirability to the bank just increased dramatically. They need you more than ever during tough economic times. Take advantage of hard times. There is *always* money available for those people whom the bank *thinks* it needs. During the tough times you will reap the rewards from cultivating the bank's interest in you. That's when you can get a home mortgage at a reasonable interest rate, when you can purchase a car for the cost of producing it. I could go on, but you get the idea. If you've played your cards right, when things go bad for the rest of the world you'll still have the keys to the bank's vault. You can buy and invest with their money and let the appreciated value of your investments pay the moneylenders back. It pays to be prepared, and in this case that means having your banker convinced he or she needs your business above all else.

The bank will investigate your finances as well as your past payment history by using their credit records and those of a credit bureau. Before you even walk into your bank for that next loan, take a trip to the credit bureau and ask to see your file. By law, credit bureaus are obligated to show you your file in its entirety. Now, some of you may be wondering, why should you do that? But does the credit bureau really know how promptly you pay your bills? If not, that alone could cost you your loan request. Credit bureaus are not totally reliable, and I don't remember ever seeing a credit report that didn't have an error or two in it. They often confuse similar names, and your credit status could be on someone else's file. Sometimes a credit bureau is lax in removing adverse information even though you may have won your case in court. There are countless possible errors, and you should see your file to check its accuracy. In an attempt to head off a problem, there's no reason to create one by telling the bank something negative regarding your past credit. In short, you're in a better position if you know exactly what's in your credit file.

If you do find incorrect information, you must inform the credit bureau, in writing, of their error and request a correction. Most bureaus will tell you that evidence of the error must be presented. This could take the form of a court order, or the like. Inform them that is their problem, and you are not going to do their work. You should also make a point that if the erroneous information is reported to a potential creditor and it costs you the loan, you have every intention of suing them. This is guaranteed to get their attention. The credit bureau knows full well that you can do just that if their erroneous data adversely affect your loan request.

On the other side of the coin, if you find that some bad news has been correctly reported, you are prepared to set the banker's mind at ease before he or she gets the credit report. Let's say, for example, that you had a judgment against you for a disputed bill. If you determine by checking at the credit bureau that this incident was picked up on your credit file, tell your banker. When applying for the loan, mention that your credit is excellent, but he may find a judgment for an unpaid bill on the credit report. Make up your own story, but you might consider saying that it was a bill that you intentionally didn't pay because the merchandise was faulty. The banker will feel much better and certainly not surprised when the report is received. You have taken a bad situation and wisely turned it into a plus. Your banker will think that you told him or her out of sheer honesty rather than out of necessity.

8

HOW TO PYRAMID THE BANK'S MONEY FOR YOUR OWN USE

One of the hardest things for an individual to do is establish a credit rating that will allow him or her to borrow money on an unsecured basis. A bank (within reason, of course) will always lend you money for a house, car, and so forth. This is the best of all situations, because the bank receives a high return on its investment while being totally secure in the knowledge that if you default, the bank doesn't lose out. If you have a good credit rating on a secured lending basis only, you have a credit rating that is virtually meaningless. The bank will give you $7,000 for that car provided you are purchasing a car worth $10,000 and have proof of insurance should you have an accident. Stated another way, if you put up $10,000 they will be more than happy to loan you $7,000 at unbelievably high rates.

The problem arises when you have that urgent need for money but no collateral. When you approach your banker with a loan request such as this, you will be amazed to find out that having successfully paid back two car loans at that bank without ever missing a payment will mean absolutely nothing. Some of you may never have had the need for a signature loan (the same as an unsecured loan), but I am sure the day will come when you will need one. You may want to start a small business and only have half the money necessary for your new venture, or possibly there may be a family crisis, medical bills, or the like. Sooner or later you will need your bank to believe in *you* and not your collateral, so you should anticipate this before it happens. This is accomplished by soothing the banker's apprehensions before they arise.

A banker's lack of respect for the average person probably stems from a preoccupation with fancy financial statements touting billion-dollar corporations. The banker would be better off paying more attention to his everyday customers. These are the important people who keep his bank open and operating. A corporation's financial statements can always be juggled to accomplish procedures that can make a sick company look completely healthy. If this wasn't the case, a bank would never lose a single dollar on a corporate loan, and yet every year banks are faced with uncollected loans of corporations that have collapsed. Even after these companies close their doors, their financial statements read like they have the key to Fort Knox. Do you remember Penn-Central, Lockheed, Chrysler, etc.? These companies, with no visual means of support, at one time still qualified for millions of dollars of extended credit, and you can't even get $2,000 using just your signature! One of the reasons that corporations are able to receive loans of staggering amounts is that the bank is greedy, and it knows that one good corporate loan can return exceptionally high interest for the bank while taking up very little time in servicing. The arithmetic is simple: Lend $2 million to one company, and the bank has replaced the equivalent of 333 individual loans at $6,000 each. A bank doesn't care one iota that it is violating the moral responsibility of its banking charter—i.e., adequately and efficiently serving their customers within their defined market area. All they care about is putting as much money out, at the highest rate possible, with the lowest possible servicing costs and risk of loss. As long as the bank services a token percentage of its customers, enough to satisfy the subjective requirements of the bank examiners, all is well. Bank management knows that they will not be bothered by governmental agencies whose responsibility is to monitor the degree of responsiveness to the community's banking needs. (See Conclusion.) As I said, a bank need only serve a small percentage of its customers in a lending area, and now I am going to show you how to make sure you are one of those being served.

You are going to borrow money even though you don't need it. You are going to do this to establish an unsecured credit rating. This is the only credit rating worth worrying about or spending any time developing. First, open up a time certificate of deposit in the highest amount you can afford and with a time span that won't be uncomfortable for you to live with until it reaches maturity. A few days later go back to the bank and apply for an unsecured loan, explaining to the loan officer that you just opened a TCD for, let's say, $1,000. Tell the officer something has come up (make up your own story if necessary) and that you need to borrow $1,000 on an unsecured basis for thirty days. The loan officer may suggest using the newly opened TCD as collateral, but at this point *you must refuse politely.* Explain that the funds in the certificate of deposit will be there for the duration of the unsecured loan. If not you would simply have to cash in the TCD and accept the high interest penalty, which you don't want to do. Remind the officer that the bank would have the right to offset at all times in case of default. (The right of offset allows the bank to confiscate any funds on deposit in its institution if you owe the bank a delinquent loan, or if the bank has just cause to feel your loan is in jeopardy, even if you have never made a late payment. It would be wise, therefore, if you are having trouble making your loan payments and still have money in your checking or savings account, to move these funds to another bank.) If the loan officer still won't agree to an unsecured loan, ask to see the president. If you still fail, cash in your TCD and move on to another bank. You wouldn't want to do business here anyway. In most cases, however, you will be successful and be granted the loan. Now take the money you borrowed from Bank X and move on to the next bank and do the exact same thing. Use as many banks as necessary to establish the line of credit you desire. You may wish to do this a few times with a number of banks, and if you can increase the amount requested each time, you will be assured that your borrowing power has been established in a fairly short time and for substantial sums.

Banks tend to use their own credit files more than those of credit bureaus, and a bank's own files carry more weight with it. In six months you could easily have a record of prompt payment with six different banks on an "unsecured" basis for, let's say, $4,000 each. When you really need the funds in the future you can acquire up to $20,000 using your signature only. This borrowing chain, *which is perfectly legal,* will cost you a few dollars in interest, but a good deal of this will be negated by the interest you've earned on your TCD at each bank. If you play it right it will cost you only a reduction in the net amount earned.

You can take this borrowing chain to any extreme you wish as long as you understand the necessity of timing when you really want to borrow money unsecured and are going to rely on your record, and not the fact that you had a TCD in excess of the previous loan. When you apply for the number of loans you need to accomplish your line of credit, you must apply to each bank on the same day, as you *must* give the banker an honest application and possibly a financial statement. If you already have a loan at two of the banks in the chain, you *must* reflect them on your application. If you don't, you are in serious trouble because you have just broken a federal law. If you have simply applied to six banks on the same day that needn't be reflected in your application even though you may receive the money the next day. We are not trying to break the law, or acquire loans we do not intend to pay back. We are simply trying to establish an unsecured lending line based on past borrowing performance.

This method is designed to assist you in obtaining money that your banker might otherwise deny you.

PART II

9

BANK SERVICES

Bank "services" are, in almost every case, overpriced and of little value to the consumer. This is not a subjective opinion but rather a simple statement of fact. More important, the customer oftentimes doesn't get what he or she bargained for, as will be explained in the example of safe-deposit boxes.

It would be redundant to take apart banks "service" by "service," but I will try to substantiate my claim by using three examples most people can relate to. Obviously banks offer certain services that could be referred to as convenient and sometimes necessary, and in those cases I have no quarrel with the bank making a fair return on their costs. What I do object to is universal overpricing and marketing a "service" in a deceptive manner. Banks are guilty as charged in this regard, as our examples will show.

SAFE-DEPOSIT BOXES

Safe deposit boxes cost an average of about $20 per year, but let's review the actual cost of the box itself. I can save you the $20 fee.

If your bank has been in existence for ten years or more, it has depreciated the entire cost of the boxes. At the same time, the bank is paying for the boxes in cash with its customers' money. There's nothing wrong with this. As I've stated before, a bank is a corporation with shareholders, and a corporation has a right and an obligation to make a fair profit on an investment. The only deception here is what the customer thinks has been purchased for $20 per year. Most people use a safe-deposit box to store valuable papers, or items that have a substantial monetary value. The papers are usually birth certificates, marriage licenses, insurance papers, etc. These items *can* be replaced, however, at some inconvenience. The items of value may be cash (some people hide money from the IRS in safe-deposit boxes), stamp collections, gold, family heirlooms, etc. These articles are not replaceable without substantial loss. Your banker will tell you that each safe-deposit box is insured for $1 million. With that kind of information you can go home and sleep at night. Or can you?

Once again, your banker has sold you a bill of goods. The sad fact is if your bank is burglarized, or their vault and its contents are destroyed by whatever cause, the insurance company isn't going to pay you a single dollar for the $5,000 in cash you have been saving, or your $15,000 stamp collection *unless you can absolutely, positively prove its existence in your safe-deposit box!* You can't accomplish this feat since they will not accept your word, or the word of your spouse, friend, etc. The insurance you were led to believe you had purchased for $20 is, in fact, nonexistent.

To get around this, you have two choices. You can buy your own vault and install it in your home. This can be accomplished for under $100 and will afford the same fire and theft protection that your safe-deposit box at the bank provides. You would need to submit a certified list of the vault's contents to your insurance agent. Your homeowner's insurance policy provides a much greater replacement possibility than does the bank's insurance. If you decide that you still want a safe-deposit box, the only way to protect your valuables is to ask your banker for a safekeeping receipt. This document would need to be updated every time you go to the box.

Therefore you are going to have to allow your banker to see exactly what you have stored in the box at each visit. This is the only way you can prove to the insurance company that you actually sustained a loss should something happen to the contents. By the way, most bankers won't want to sign a safe-keeping receipt even after reviewing the contents of your box, because your banker knows the implications of his signature in your possession i.e., he now has obligated the bank *really* to be liable for any loss you may incur. His reluctance in this situation will further substantiate my claim that a safe-deposit box is not as "safe" as your banker would have you believe.

Banks always imply that no one can get into your safe-deposit box except yourself, since two keys are needed, yours and the bank's. This is just not true. A person can pop the box's lock in under thirty seconds using nothing more than a regular screwdriver. Not much safety in that, is there? The only real safety factor is the bank's vault itself, which houses the boxes. But if the bank vault is older and smaller, it can also be broken into relatively easily by a professional burglar. But leaving crime aside, there are legal ways to get into your safety deposit box without your permission. It is very easy for the IRS or state tax authority to obtain a court order permitting the box to be drilled, and have the contents reviewed and possibly confiscated. So if you are hiding anything, make sure you have your safe deposit box out of town and most definitely not where you do your normal banking or maintain other accounts. A court order to enter a safe-deposit box is valid only if the location of the box is known.

One more important fact on this subject, and it may very well be the saddest. A safe-deposit box maintained jointly in two names (yours and your spouse's, for example) can be a potential problem. If the bank becomes aware that one of the individuals is deceased, the bank is obligated, by law, to prohibit access to the box by *anyone* until the surviving party produces a certified copy of the death certificate along with appropriate tax releases. This holds true for all bank accounts held jointly. So if you have valuables or money in a jointly held safe-deposit box, make certain all parties are aware that it is urgent to visit the bank *before* the obituary is published and to close any joint account. Of course, if you have your safe-deposit box in another town, the chances are considerably less that the bank will see the obituary or be aware of the death. But the account should still be closed as soon as possible.

MONEY ORDERS, CASHIER'S CHECKS, AND TRAVELER'S CHECKS

Typically, a money order costs $.50 to $1.00. The fee for a cashier's check is approximately $2.00. These appear to be fairly reasonable costs, at face value. However, a closer look will reveal that the bank is making an exorbitant amount on even this simple transaction. Imagine what the bank is doing to you on the "larger ticket items."

Let's assume you purchase a cashier's check for $2,000.00 and use the check to purchase a used car in a private sale. You purchase the check on Friday and buy the car on Saturday. The seller can't get to the bank on Saturday because it's too late. So the seller deposits the check on Monday morning. Typically, the check will take a minimum of two to three days to clear back to the bank of origin. This means that the bank has had the use of the money for six days. This is referred to as "making use of float." (Traveler's checks of all kinds generate millions of dollars per year based on the same principle.) Although it's not important here to understand the entire bank clearing system, it does help to understand that the bank is once again using your money to make a profit and at the same time charging you money up front. Let's take this simple transaction and run a cost analysis to see the actual cost of that $2,000.00 cashier's check.

Cashier's check for $2,000.00	Fee, $2.00
Interest earned by bank	
($2,000.00 × 13% × 6 days)	4.27
Total earned by bank	6.27

Minus cost of the check printing	.13
Minus cost of handling and processing (including computer costs)	.25
Net profit to bank	**$5.89**

NOTE: The interest earned by the bank is based on an investment of monies on a daily basis, which banks do regularly. The 13 percent rate in this example is a reasonable estimate, even though a bank's daily investment rate has been as high as 22 percent in the recent past.

Once again I want to emphasize that the bank has done nothing illegal here. I mention the situation of up-front charges to the customer along with float earnings because it is one more method a bank uses to make money using your money. My only complaint is that the monies expended by you to perform everyday financial transactions are taken to the extreme by the bank's profit centers. You spent only $2.00 for the cashier's check, so it sounds like I'm making a big deal out of little. But separate the expended dollars from the principal involved and then realize that this is only a small part of the bank's plan to make every dollar possible from your needs. To prove my point, let's see what rate of interest the bank made on your money in this very simple transaction.

The bank expended $.38 for a total of six days. For that investment it earned $6.27. That is the equivalent of a return to the bank of 100,375 percent! You would think with that kind of return the bank would provide the check free. In a later chapter I'll show you how to accomplish this, but right now I will simply tell you that banking services are outrageously overpriced.

All bank services such as money orders, cashier's checks, traveler's checks, etc., work on the same principle. A quick review of these "services" was necessary so you don't feel too guilty when I offer a way to receive these services free. They will be free, but as you will see, they still provide the bank with sizable return on a paltry investment.

OTHER SERVICE CHARGES

There are several other ways a bank can pick your pocket. Let's start with loan late charges.

First, I have no sympathy for people who don't pay obligations on time (except in extreme situations that make it virtually impossible to meet the terms of a loan agreement). Since the bank gives you ten days' "grace" on receiving your payment before a late charge is assessed, under normal circumstances you have more than enough time to make your payment. Also, let's remember that late charges are assessed only on installment loans. On single-payment notes you are charged one more day's interest for each day the payment is late. Mortgages are a different matter, since a late payment affects the amortization schedule, causing complications that I won't elaborate on now. Let's assume you didn't take my advice on avoiding installment loans, and for some reason you are late with your installment payment. The bank is going to charge you $15.00. As an example, we'll assume that your payment due was $240.00, and you were twelve days late. What rate did the bank charge you for making your payment late? Well, since they "lost" the ability to invest your $240.00 for twelve days, they did run up some costs in printing the late notice, additional computer charges, the clerical staff's cost of processing, etc. It is fair that they recoup these fees— a total of approximately $1.52. Yet they are charging you $15.00, which is a return on their investment of 30016.44 percent. You can see, once again, the bank has taken advantage of you. All I am suggesting is that the banks play fair and return to you what they are more than willing to take. Would your bank be willing to pay you $15.00 if you made your installment payment 12 days early? Of course not. But why shouldn't a bank do this? A banker would say it all balances out. I say it is a rip-off, and the customer bears the brunt.

Now let's turn our attention to one of a bank's favorite charges, the overdraft charge. Again, I want to say I don't condone habitually overdrawing your checking account.

Writing bad checks knowingly is a crime. Granted, it's a misdemeanor that is rarely enforced, but it still is against the law. If you deliberately write a bad check you probably get off easy when the bank charges you $10.00, but how about those times that you simply made an honest error, or your deposit was made the same day the check was presented to the bank for payment? Because of computer lag time, your deposit sometimes is not reflected on the bank's records until the following day, or perhaps two days later if a weekend intervenes. Even under these circumstances, the bank will charge you $10.00 and return the check. The result is that the bank lost the investment of the amount of the check for one day. To illustrate, we'll say that the check was written for $200.00. The bank's loss of investment was $.07 ($200.00 × 13 percent, divided by 365 days × 1 day). This, together with computer notice and other costs—and I am being more than generous—totals $.50. Yet the bank is charging you $10.00. This time they made a return on their "investment" of 730,000 percent. Banks don't mind using your money for their benefit, but Lord help the poor customer who attempts to return the favor. Again, you shouldn't overdraw your account intentionally, but that doesn't give a bank the right to take advantage of your honest error.

The money banks make this way can add up fast. I once worked for a bank that was highly profitable, yet the bank's total profits were less than the bank's total charges for overdrafts! I am not implying that the bank's profits are not the net result of numerous financial decisions minus the basic cost of doing business. However, in this specific case the bank would have been losing money on a yearly basis if it weren't for the income generated by overdraft charges.

Did it ever occur to you that the charge for an overdraft on a $1,000.00 check is the same as it is for a $25.00 check? The reason for this strange inequity is that the bank makes so much money from this service charge that it really doesn't matter what the one-day "loss" is. In Chapter 14 I will show you a way of avoiding overdraft charges, but for now understand that these changes are another indication of how a bank legally takes advantage of its customers.

There are numerous other banking services I could review, but I would be beating a dead horse. My objective is not to take the banking system apart service by service but rather to give you enough general information for an understanding of the system as a whole.

10

THE BANK'S "GIFT" AT CHRISTMAS

One of the packaging gimmicks banks have used over the years to fatten their coffers is the Christmas Club. This "service" usually takes the form of a coupon book that reflects equal payments in an amount you have selected, such as $10.00 per week. The payments are normally spread over fifty weeks with you making the first forty-nine payments, and some banks making the final payment, providing you have made the full forty-nine prior payments. In effect, the bank is paying you $10.00 interest for the use of money you have saved for the express purpose of Christmas expenses. There are various other club accounts designed for different purposes and that function along the same lines.

Before I discuss the real cost of this "service," it must be noted that many banks no longer offer Christmas Clubs (or have changed their packaging), because it has become apparent to the public that the practice is blatantly unfair. Nevertheless, it is worth going into, since many smaller banks are still picking their customers' pockets using the Christmas Club.

By your making payments of $10.00 per week, the bank does not have the full use of your money for the entire fifty weeks. On average, it can be said that the bank has the use of approximately half of your money for fifty weeks. So for forty-nine payments at $10.00 each, the bank has the use of approximately $245.00 for forty-nine weeks. In return they are willing to pay you $10.00 *provided* you make all the preceding payments. Miss only one payment and you have forfeited your $10.00. Assuming that you make all your payments, let's see how the bank's gain is your loss.

First, how much do you think you would have earned had you simply made a $10.00 per week deposit into a regular savings account? The interest for fifty weeks amounts to $12.36. Even at this paltry return rate, you would earn $2.36 *more* than the bank is willing to pay *if* you made all your Christmas Club payments. That's the simple analysis based on the amount of interest differential gain on your Christmas Club. Since the bank has the use of only half of the funds for forty-nine weeks, its earnings at 13 percent daily return is $30.62. This could be lower, or it could be much higher, since the daily return rate has gone as high as 22 percent. Let's prepare a cost analysis:

Bank gross earnings at 13%	30.62
Minus last payment (interest)	10.00
Minus cost of coupon book for Christmas Club	1.35 (approx.)
Minus the cost of processing coupons	1.87
Net return to bank on your $10.00 per week Christmas Club account	$17.40

Of course, the bank has a right and an obligation to earn money on your deposits. But I object to packaging techniques that are designed solely to give a customer an erroneous impression and to take advantage of his or her ignorance. Conceptually there is nothing wrong with a Christmas Club. What is wrong is that the bank, by its silence, steals some of your money up front (*the difference between the interest you could have earned in a regular savings account, minus the actual amount of the last payment made by the bank*). The bank then makes an inordinately high return on its investment, the bank's actual expense divided by its profit, as seen in the following table:

The bank's total expense for your Christmas Club	$13.22
The bank's net earnings	17.40
The bank's net return on their investment of time and service	131.61%

Although these figures are fairly incriminating to the bank, we are making the assumption that you made the forty-ninth payment. What happens if you didn't? The net return to the bank, in dollars, then jumps to $27.40, and the return escalates to 207.26 percent!

You are probably wondering why I am making such a big deal about such a small amount of money. If you take my advice and never use a Christmas Club, I have saved you only $2.36 in our example and about $12.00 if you had missed only one payment. But let's look at it from the bank's point of view: Well over half of the Christmas Club account customers in a given bank will not make all their payments and therefore will lose the last payment. To see the overall effect in a medium-size bank, let's use the following example and see the results:

Deposit of $50 million Christmas Club deposits based on .7% of total deposits	$350,000.00
Number of Christmas Club accounts at $500 each	700
Profit on half of the clubs at $17.40 each	6,090.00
Profit on half of the clubs at $27.40 each	9,590.00
Total profits to bank	15,680

You can see how a small amount of extra income can quickly accumulate in a bank that deals with a large volume. The bank has to make only a few extra bucks per account to arrive at a large total figure. A high-performance bank of the size in our example would typically earn $500,000.00 per year. With very little effort and a great deal of planned confusion or deception, they have made 3.136 percent of their total expected earnings on the Christmas Club function alone. This entire principle works exactly the same in those instances where the bank offers a premium for opening a Christmas Club. The cost of the premium (to the bank) is made up by offering the customer less interest (or no interest) than they could receive in another kind of account. (This is an important point to remember whenever your bank offers you a "Free" premium. The ultimate cost of that "Freebie" is coming out of your pocket; in some cases the bank even makes money.) It's just the bank's way of wishing you and yours a very Merry Christmas.

11

"CONVENIENCE" SERVICES: VERY CONVENIENT FOR THE BANK

As just one example of how banks offer "convenience" at tremendous benefit to themselves, let's review the "service" of collecting your real-estate taxes. This will give you another piece of information in forming your judgment on the banking industry and will help show you how you can use your own system to beat their system.

As you well know, every year local government and taxing authorities assess a tax on your property. Depending on the value of your home, the tax rate, how quickly it escalates, and the length of time you retain possession of your property, it is quite possible that you will pay more in real-estate taxes over time than you paid for your home in the first place. Not surprisingly, banks have figured out a way to get a piece of the action.

The only "service" banks are offering here is convenience, for whatever that's worth. In return, they once again use your money. As an example, I'll use my own situation. We live in a modest home for which we paid $51,000 six years ago. During the first year our taxes were less then $700. This year they escalated to $1,250, which are paid in two equal install-ments on the last possible day. (Always pay your taxes of any kind on the last day allowable.)

The bank collects the money and then remits the funds to the county treasurer or clerk on the scheduled date. This may be on a biweekly basis, or sometimes every six weeks. For the sake of discussion, let's use a midpoint of four weeks to illus-trate the following bank computation. Remember, however, that the bank has opportunities for daily investments that you don't.

Taxes collected	$625.00
Return to bank ($625.00 × 13%, divided by 52 weeks × 4 weeks)	6.25
Total return to bank ($6.25 × 2 payments)	12.50
Less cost of service (total of six minutes teller time; average $3.60 per hour divided by 60 minutes × 6)	.36
Net to bank	$12.14

You might think that I am making a big deal about a small sum of money here. After all, I didn't pay the $12.14 out of my own pocket. You're right, but there's more to it than that.

This is, at the very least, a "hidden" cost of the real-estate tax. Were you aware of the bank's ability to use the money collected? Maybe yes, maybe no, but the real issue here is that the bank has one set of rules for the customer's neces-sities and another set of rules for the attainment of bank earn-ings. You have, in effect, loaned your bank money for its use with no return to you. Does the bank offer you money on the same basis? Absolutely not! A bank will charge you every penny it can, whenever it can, and for every single day you use its money. In some cases, you're even charged additional interest. For instance, if you take out a loan on Friday night, you're still charged for the full day, and more often than not, you are also charged for the day you pay the loan back. So the bank is receiving two full days of interest even though you did not have the use of the money for those two days. The bank astutely realizes that a few dollars here and there can add up.

So, the next time you feel that you are getting a convenience service from the bank without any cost to you, think again.

12

SLAYING THE FLOAT MONSTER

Banks create money out of thin air. They don't print their own money as they did in the past, but they create it nevertheless. They accomplish this by making loans, and that "creates" money. Bank accounting is directly contrary to normal accounting principles: Since deposits are accepted on a fiduciary basis, the bank owes money to depositors. The cash (deposits) that would normally become an asset to a corporation become a liability to the bank. Loans, on the other hand, are owed to the bank and are accounted an asset. This is drastically oversimplified, but it will give you enough background to understand the following scenario.

The bank loans $10,000.00 to Mr. Jones. He signs the loan papers and in return receives a cashier's check in the amount of the principal obligation. On the bank's books, both total assets and liabilities have increased $10,000.00, even though no money has changed hands. The bank has at this point created $10,000.00. This may not seem very impressive until you realize that every credit extension in this country does the same thing. Because of this, billions of dollars in the nation's money supply are nonexistent at any given moment.

If Mr. Jones was purchasing a car, for example, he would

leave the bank and go to the car dealership. The car dealer would accept the check and deposit it in *his* bank. His bank would clear the check back to the lending bank. This process, depending on when the loan was made, the day of the week, when the car dealer makes his deposit, etc., could take as much as a week. At that point (and only at that point) would the lending bank have to pay for the check. That means in this instance the bank had the use of the funds, in that they were charging Mr. Jones interest from the time they handed him the check, for seven days. In the process they made $15.33 ($10,000.00 × 8 percent divided by 365 × 7 days). This "loan float" when applied to a bank's loan portfolio adds up to hundreds of thousands of dollars annually in bigger banks. Is this fair to the consumer? Most assuredly not. If you "created" your own money as the banks do, you would probably go to jail under the deceptive practices section of your state's laws.

Customers can create their own money, but it's illegal. It's called check kiting. Basically it works like this. The customer opens up, let's say, three accounts at three different banks— banks X, Y, and Z. You deposit a $1,000.00 check in bank X, drawn on bank Y. To cover that check you write a $1,200.00 check drawn on bank Z and deposit it in bank Y, and so on, and so on. Even if you could at any time pay all the money created by the check kite, the scheme is illegal. I haven't told you enough here for a check kite to work, and in addition the bank has in its computer system a program to weed out kite suspects. A kite quickly becomes unruly and the average person is an odds-on favorite to get caught, so I wouldn't recommend it. Interestingly enough, though, kite "experts" are successful quite often for unbelievable sums of money. They are able to accomplish this because of flaws in the clearing system, a fatal flaw in most bank's computer sytems, and a bank staff (including officers) that is unprofessional and financially uneducated.

The point here is that banks create money every day, and they make great profits in the process. "Loan float" is, in my mind, every bit as unethical as check kiting. The difference is that banks make money with their scheme—the customer who in principle does the same thing with a check kite can go to jail.

The bank's standard float policy is far more damaging to the customer than "loan float," as there is much more money involved. In today's market almost every bank has an internal policy of how they "pay" your checks as they clear the bank. Typically, banks accept your deposit checks on a ten-day hold. Sometimes it's a ten-"business"-day hold, which means two calendar weeks. The bank then considers the deposit to be in your account balance. Only then will they let you draw funds against the account. Checks that arrive at the bank that need that deposit to be paid will be returned NSF or UN-COLLECTED FUNDS. A substantial fee usually accompanies the return, and you will get a notice that the fee has been assessed against your account.

In fact, however, most checks clear the system within two to three days, some in as little as one. Obviously, the bank now has the use of your money for seven days, and they invest these funds to increase their profits. Let's use an example to show how this works. We will use a bank daily investment rate of 13 percent. We will also use an actual clearing time of three days.

Date	Checks Amount	Deposits	Account Balance	Balance Available to Pay Checks	Bank Float to Use
8/1/83			$5,000	$5,000	$5,000
8/3/83		$2,500	7,500	5,000	5,000
8/6/83					7,500
8/9/83	$4,000		3,500	1,000	3,500
8/10/83	1,500		2,000	−500	2,000

On 8/10 your check would be sent back NSF and you would be charged a fee (typically $10.00) even though you still had a $2,000 balance.

| 8/11/83 | | | 2,000 | 2,000 | 2,000 |

During the time of our example the bank charged you a $10.00 fee for an NSF check that wasn't, caused you the humiliation of having the check returned to the payee, and in the process made $19.58 interest by investing *your* money (total balance of $55,000 divided by 11 equals $5,000; $5,000 × 13% divided by 365 × 11 equals $19.58). The total the bank earned was $29.58 (interest plus NSF charge). Even in these days of NOW accounts—the payment of interest for checking accounts—this figure seems exorbitant, and the bank has no right to make this money.

Bankers will tell you that they need this added clearing time to assure that deposited checks won't be returned. In rare cases checks are returned, but the percentage is minuscule (1 percent) compared to the number of checks that are paid as agreed. I've made my point. It's time to show you how to get even.

I have implored people for years, for a number of different reasons, to sue their banks. In a later chapter I discuss suing the bank in small claims court. Here I want to address the moral issue of suing the bank for a large sum of money even though you "lost" only a few dollars. Customers have to start doing this because the deck is stacked, and until banks lose huge sums in court they are going to continue to set arbitrary policies (such as the ten-day hold on deposits) that are stealing your money.

I am proud to report that the *Chicago Tribune* ran a story titled "Bank Sued Over Check Policy" with the subhead "Depositor Challenges Continental Holding Period." The story says, in part: "A lady by the name of Marianne Dreier has sued Continental Illinois National Bank of Chicago for the sum of . . . $10 million in punitive damages from Continental and actual damage equal to the amount of earnings realized by the bank from its check holding policy over the last ten years. It asks that the bank be required to distribute that money to all depositors affected by the policy. It also seeks an injunction to prevent the bank from continuing the practice."

Another quote from the article is worth noting: "We have several checks showing on the backs that they were cleared within a day or two," said Dreier's attorney, Larry D. Drury. "They were written by her employer, which is located only two blocks away from Continental. But when she wanted to make a withdrawal, the bank said there were no funds in the account."

Obviously, this case will take years to resolve. My guess is that Ms. Dreier's attorney is working on a contingency basis, which means that he will earn a fee only from what he can win on the suit. Ms. Dreier would therefore not have to pay him out of her pocket. Whether she wins the case is not that important. It would be great if she did because of the precedent that would be set, but even if she loses, the bank is going to have to spend thousands, possibly hundreds of thousands, in legal fees. Even if the bank wins, I would guess they will rethink their check-holding policy. My recommendation to you is: Research your bank's policy to see what their check-holding policy is. If you find it unreasonable, find a lawyer who will take your case on contingency, and sue the bank. In Ms. Dreier's case the unstated amount (equal to the amount the bank earned on this policy over the last ten years) must be staggering. Ms. Dreier may, when this case is decided, be a multimillionaire, and all because she had the guts to fight the system.

You can do the same. Even if you lose, you win. If you're on contingency the worst that can happen is that you have cost the bank the legal fees to clear themselves; in effect you've gotten even. The point is that if each bank in this country got sued three or four times for each of their unfair practices they would soon go back to the intent of their bank charter and start serving the community.

13

YOU WERE ON TIME, BUT YOU WERE LATE— AND OTHER "ERRORS"

Banks function as paper clearinghouses. The average customer would be amazed at the number of clearing items even a small bank handles during a typical banking day. To combat the paper onslaught banks have learned to make good use of the computer. Without computers, banking as we know it today would cease to exist. Computers that have the capability to process the number of items a bank has, and route them properly, are very expensive. There is the cost of buying the system, the costs of operation, housing, and repair, and the cost of the personnel necessary to monitor and program. Because of these and other reasons, the vast majority of banks use a computer center, or that of a correspondent bank large enough to afford its own computer to process the daily work. This means that most banks have to ship daily work out every night and then receive the results of yesterday's work the following morning. Depending on where a particular bank is located and its proximity to the computer center, many banks have had to reschedule their workday to coincide with computer and shipping availability. The upshot is that many banks have been forced to establish a cutoff time for the day's work. Some banks, even though they are open later, have a cutoff of 2:00 P.M. for that day's business. Therefore, even though a bank willingly accepts your deposit or loan payment on a particular day, there is a good chance that the transaction will not be credited to your account until the following day. When you add a weekend, holiday, or day off into this flow of work, it can play havoc with your account and loan payments. For example, let's say that your bank has a cutoff of 2:00 P.M., and you make a loan payment on Tuesday that is due on Tuesday at 2:45 P.M. Let's further assume that your bank is closed on Wednesday (as many are). Since the bank has a 2:00 P.M. cutoff for Tuesday's work, your loan payment will not be reflected until Wednesday. However, since the bank is closed Wednesday, the payment will not be included in the work until Thursday. The bank loan officer, unless he saw you make the deposit, will not be aware of your payment until Friday morning. If, in our example, Tuesday was the last day of your ten-day grace period, you are going to be hit with a late charge because of the delay in processing your payment. In addition, your loan history file on the computer will now show, from that day forward, a late payment by you. In all fairness, your credit rating should never have been so affected.

Similarly, a deposit delayed in this way can cause a check to be returned. In fact, the bank had your deposit before the check was presented for payment—but checks could be sent back for insufficient funds, causing embarrassment to you and possibly adversely affecting your credit rating. In addition, you may have incurred an insufficient-amount charge for one or more checks. This money is immediately debited to your account, and you are going to have to fight to get it back. Because of this problem, most banks have the tellers advance the date on their machines at 2:00 P.M., if they have a cutoff time, so your deposit receipt on Tuesday at 2:45 P.M. will show a date of Thursday. This helps cover their service deficiency.

You will find that most banks, when confronted with this delay in processing, will refund the overdraft charge or late-payment charge. The real problem, as I see it, is that the bank may have damaged your credit rating for no valid reason. Generally the bank will offer to do nothing to correct the damage caused. To compound an already bad situation, the bank has probably also created a bookkeeping problem for you. In most cases it is not until days after the fact that you become aware that something has gone wrong. The bank knows that the vast majority of its customers will simply pay the charges and never say anything. I would estimate, based on my own experience, that about 15 percent of late charges are completely unjustifiable.

If this is correct, the following example will show that the effect on the bank's total revenue is staggering. Let's take a $30 million small-town bank and apply the 15 percent to their income accounts that cover these charges:

Approximate overdraft charges per month	$ 5,500.00
Approximate overdraft charges per year	66,000.00
15% due to computer and service lag time	9,900.00
Approximate loan late charges per year	48,000.00
Approximate 15% error factor	7,200.00
Total 15% error income factor	17,100.00

A high-performance bank of this size would generate approximately $300,000 in income. By error income, as I prefer to call it, the bank has generated 5.7 percent of its net yearly income by having inadequate systems. The bank is, in effect, offering service that is inaccurate, outmoded, and overpriced—and then making this a profit base! Many bankers would argue this point, and they would offer all sorts of statistics in an attempt to convince you that this is not happening at their institution. They may very well be right, in select situations. As I have mentioned, this does not occur at every bank. But it does happen, and my example may be understated in a good many cases. Some banks have solved this problem by having a direct link to their computer (referred to as "on-line"), which then reflects immediately the true current balance in any account. This approach is totally fair, but unfortunately it is used only in a small number of banks.

If you receive a charge for a "service" you feel is unfair or in error, go into the bank and state your case. Settle for nothing less than a fair resolution to your problem. As long as banks continue to receive little or no criticism in this area they are not going to spend the extra money necessary for updated computer programs. Bankers certainly are not going to relinquish a tidy income base just because they are creating problems for you.

As previously mentioned, another area where banks *transfer* their errors to customers is in the case of returned checks. Due to collection time and the individual bank's computer service, it is quite possible that you may make a deposit before a check clears the bank. Sometimes (though rarely) the bank makes a mistake and your check is returned erroneously. Most people may complain to their bank if this occurs, and the bank dutifully apologizes, then leaves the customer with the problem of explaining the error to the company or individual who received the "bad" check. The problem here is that the recipient of the check probably won't believe your story, no matter how true it may be. To the recipient, you are a problem. They may even require that you pay cash from that day forward. The solution here is simple, but rarely does a customer take advantage of the opportunity. Request that the bank issue you a letter explaining to the company or individual who received your check that it was a bank error. Furthermore, the letter should state that their error should not adversely affect your credit with them. Be certain to retain a copy of the letter, because you may use it later if additional problems arise with the bank. Simply stated, if your bank makes an error, insist that it admit it in *writing*. A number of good credit ratings have been destroyed by bank errors. Once this happens it is almost impossible to correct the situation with the credit bureau. Bank errors, such as returned checks that were good, or erroneous reporting on your payment record, are an excellent basis for a substantial lawsuit if you are denied credit as a result. It is unfortunate that more consumers don't pursue this. If financial centers were hit with enough losses due to their own errors, the integrity of business and the respect for an individual's credit rating would be preserved. Remember, when *you* are in error with your bank—making a late loan payment, or overdrawing your checking account—you are made to pay for your error. In all fairness, you must now take every opportunity to return the favor when your bank is in error.

Another service that often causes problems for the customer is the stop-payment order. Stopping payment over the phone is good for only fourteen days, unless authorized in writing within that period. A signed stop-payment order will legally protect you. The problem arises when you order a stop payment too late and the check has already been paid. If, for example, the stop payment was ordered on Wednesday and the check was paid on Tuesday, the bank has fulfilled its obligation. Quite often the bank will accept a stop-payment order in the morning, and the check is paid by a teller that same afternoon. The bank will tell the customer that the law allows a "reasonable" time for activating the stop payment, but unfortunately the check was paid before all the relevant employees were notified. This is a judgment made by the bank that is in its best interest but certainly not in yours. A "reasonable" time for enacting a stop-payment order is ambiguous. There are many different sizes of banks in this country, and it should be obvious that it would take longer for a bank with $10 billion and ten branches to cover all bases than it would be for a hometown bank with only fifteen employees. In the latter case, it should be expected that if the bank did its job efficiently, a stop-payment order would be completely in effect within minutes. This is why you must receive a copy of the stop-payment order if you request one in person. In the case of a telephone order for a stop payment, you must note the time you called and whom you spoke to at the bank. My experience has been that as many as five out of one hundred stop-payment orders are handled improperly by banks, and these checks have been paid. One of the many ways the bank transfers their error to the customer is by claiming that erroneous information was provided on the stop-payment order. If there was erroneous information, this technically gets the bank off the hook. I know of one case where the bookkeeping department of a bank was told to make at least one error, no matter how minor, on every stop-payment order processed. After the customer signed the order, the bank was off the hook if the check slipped through. The bank, I would assume, still made every effort to handle every stop-payment order properly, but they had left themselves an out in case of error.

Banks are very sensitive about the subject of stop-payment orders. The law states that should a check be paid after the bank has received proper notice of a stop-payment order, the bank has just "purchased" the check in its entirety. In a smaller bank, payment of a $5,000 to $10,000 check could easily represent 10 percent of the bank's yearly net profit. Therefore, the bank will do whatever is necessary within the letter of the law to make the customer pay for its own mistake. Since the customer usually is uninformed in this area, the bank is more often than not completely successful. Remember, if a bank is remiss on a stop-payment order, it is the bank's problem, not yours. This, of course, does not relieve you of legal responsibility to the person to whom the check was made payable, but the check itself, and the amount paid out in error, falls back on the bank. You may have to take legal action to prove this point, and the bank knows this. This is one of the reasons that banks in general are not responsive legally or morally to their customers. They know that governmental agencies will do absolutely nothing, and if it goes to court, the banks no doubt can afford better legal representation than you can. So it becomes advantageous for the bank (if it has made an error on a stop-payment order that would be substantially costly) to go through a court procedure and wait it out. These cases can go on for years, and the bank hopes that you will become discouraged and give up before it has to pay for the mistake. Unfortunately, banks are successful more often than not.

What about stopping payment on a bank money order or cashier's check? Most bankers will tell you that you can't do this—but don't believe them. *These items can be stopped,* and if the bank states a contrary policy, you are being misled. The *only* instrument that cannot be stopped is a certified check. (I strongly recommend that you never use this method of payment, for this reason.) Banks don't like stop-payment orders on one of their checks because it entails additional work and diligence by their staff. Depending on the computer service used, it may mean that the only way a bank check can be stopped is through a manual screening of all incoming bank checks. This process greatly increases the possibility of error, so some banks tell the customer that a stop-payment order cannot be applied to a cashier's check. If you never signed a stop-payment order, it's simply your word against the bank's. In this case you are going to lose. If the bank won't honor your request for a stop-payment order on a bank check, make sure to return with someone else to serve as a witness and go through the same process of applying for the stop-payment order again. If you are forced to go to court to collect the money you had wished stopped, at least you will have some basis for a case.

You may find that you have been the victim of a forgery on your checking account, and if this is the case, it is assumed that you would immediately inform your bank. The law here is quite explicit. The bank is required to have on file actual signatures of all its depositors, and to verify each check as it clears the bank. Due to the overwhelming volume of checks that a bank handles per day, it has been necessary to establish a minimum dollar amount before the signature is scrutinized. The minimum generally has been established at $500, indicating that all checks written for less than $500 will not be screened for potential forgery. Ironically, checks below $500 are the ones most frequently paid erroneously. Banks have set this minimum because it is felt losses of less than $500 can be absorbed more economically than if they had to pay for the additional labor to screen adequately each check paid by the bank. Consequently, the professional "paperhangers" (forgers) can be very successful if they don't get too greedy per check. If a forger is really good at his or her profession, the forger isn't concerned with the screening cutoff point, because a bank employee is not apt to discover the forgery until the customer comes in to complain. But in any case, payment of a forged check is the bank's loss.

If the loss is small, the bank will, in most cases, simply have you fill out an affidavit of forgery and reimburse the money wrongly paid from your account. If the forged check is substantial, you are about to be the victim of the fastest shuffle you've ever seen!

Again, you have to realize that a $5,000 error by the bank could represent 10 percent of a small bank's total net earnings for the year. Rest assured that bank officers in such a situation will stop at nothing to make their error your problem. There are many different ways this is accomplished. The bank has very little respect for your assets and even less for your intelligence. The first thing the bank will attempt is to convince you that the problem was all your fault. You lost the checks. You didn't report the loss as soon as you should have. It must have been one of your friends, or a family member who forged it, if the checks weren't lost or stolen. The bank will have to call the police if you pursue the matter. The bank officer will suggest that it would be better for you if you dropped your complaint. You may be told to go to the police, since it's not the bank's problem. If it is a really good forgery, they may insist that it is your signature and inform you that it is up to you to prove otherwise. There are so many approaches to this problem that it would be impossible to outline them all. But I think you are getting the idea. *No matter what your banker says, if they paid a forged check it is their problem, and you are entitled to be reimbursed immediately after filling out the appropriate forms.* SETTLE FOR NOTHING LESS!

Forgery can also occur in a savings account. This gives the bank another vehicle for trying to lessen its level of responsibility. Most savings accounts involve a passbook or certificate. The bank will, after being informed of the forgery, submit the argument that it must have been with your knowledge that the passbook was presented, or certainly you must have known about the withdrawal. The bank's arguments may sound logical, but don't fall for them. You didn't participate in the forgery, and the bank *must* reimburse you for the payout. Furthermore, they must pay you immediately. You may have to cause a scene, but stick to your guns and you will receive the funds. It should be mentioned, in all fairness, that most banks will not put you through all this and will face up to their obligation. Unfortunately, a few banks will try to make you feel like a criminal before you are paid one dime for a bank error.

14

OWN YOUR OWN BANK

The title of this chapter may sound a bit farfetched, and it is a figure of speech. You're not actually going to own a bank, but it certainly is going to seem that way.

Mr. Average Nice Guy generally establishes a relationship on the bank's terms, which puts him on the defensive. The typical scenario consists of having to convince your banker that you are indeed worthy to be granted a loan. You then must pay all incidental charges, and you are obligated to do your banking during the hours set by the bank, etc. They set the rules; you blindly obey. This in itself is amazing when you consider that without you and other customers like you, there would be no bank. Banks need you, but you're often treated by them as though you were a second-class citizen. Did you ever notice that successful people, by reputation alone, receive preferential treatment? It really doesn't matter what the facts actually are, but rather what people believe them to be. You could be dead broke, but if you have the reputation or appearance of being successful, you will still be treated like a VIP. Recognizing this fundamental aspect of human nature can be used to your advantage even in the cold, cruel world of financial relationships.

There is one other human frailty that should be recognized if you are to be truly successful in dealing with your banker. People in general and bankers in particular are greedy. If a banker has even the slightest indication that he can make a few bucks off a customer, he will bend over backward to afford that customer the kind of service that should have been provided in the first place. Collectively, bankers are a lazy lot. However they are still under constant pressure to have the bank grow and be profitable. A banker is accountable to his or her board of directors, a group of local citizens that usually have no idea of the inner workings of the bank and yet unabashedly accept $100 per hour for their participation in board meetings. As long as the bank's management can keep the board happy, bank executives can continue to be unproductive while still collecting large weekly salary checks. To keep up this charade, your banker needs the big-deal customer, while the average customer is generally regarded as a chronic pain in the neck.

Before we proceed any further, let's talk about the type of bank you should be dealing with. *Never* use the services of a big bank. If you live in a large city, select the smallest bank in your area. The same principle applies in all cases, even in a small town. A large bank doesn't really need your business (regardless of what the advertising says), and in most cases the staff will, through a lack of attention and courtesy, make that clear. With the smaller bank you at least have a fighting chance of being recognized as a potential "big shot." After you have made your choice of the smallest bank, it's time to establish your accounts.

Your first visit to the bank should be made wearing your best clothes. This may sound trivial, but it is *very* important. Take *all* the money you can lay your hands on—$5,000 or more is best. If such an amount is not immediately available, pool all your money from all sources, even borrow from a friend or family member for just a few days. Now walk into the bank of your choosing wearing your Sunday best. Talk to the person at the front desk and ask to see the president. If he or she is not available, leave your name and a message that you will return, or better yet, leave your number and ask to have the president call you back. Tell the person taking the message that this is in reference to opening a number of accounts. (Before going into the bank to meet with the president for the first time, you *must* obtain the names of two or three directors. This can be done by calling the bank the week prior to your visit and acquiring their names, or by scanning the bank's quarterly published reports. The reason for this will become clear shortly.) Introduce yourself to the president and say that you have accounts in substantial money amounts at another bank and that you are considering moving them because you are not happy with the service. The president will love to hear this, since banks are most competitive with one another. Don't belittle the competition too much, or you may appear to be a troublesome customer. Simply say that despite your substantial account balances the other bank is still charging you for all the services you feel you should receive free. Then tell the president that you were talking to Director Smith, or was it Director Jones, or Director Johnson? Appear to be unsure exactly which director recommended that you come in to talk to the president. The director was sure that with your kind of deposits something could be worked out. This approach, which may not fit everyone's personality accomplishes two important goals in your quest for free banking services. First, it puts the bank president on notice that you know some of the people the president reports to (and he or she always has to worry about their egos), and second, you have made the connection in the president's mind without that person being able to pursue the matter further at that point. This was the reason why you casually mentioned more than one director's name.

If the banker wants to know specifically what deposit figure you are considering transferring to this bank, I suggest stretching the truth to this person. Do this in an amount you feel comfortable with; you can indicate a large amount but keep the exact amount vague. You might say that you have several hundred thousand dollars in investments that will be coming due at different times and would be willing to move them to this bank if you were to receive a number of assurances. Continue by explaining that you want a NOW checking account, but you don't feel you should pay for the checks. You'd like all other additional services free, such as cashier's checks, money orders, safe-deposit box, traveler's checks, and so forth. Since the banker won't be there every time you come into the bank, you would appreciate the banker providing you with a short letter you can show to the bank's staff whenever the need arises. Now is the time to play your trump card. Hand the banker the $5,000 (or more) and say that you would like to open up a *small* checking account with these funds and that you will add to it as your investments come due. Again, you are taking advantage of greed, and most likely *your* conditions will be met. At this point say that you would like to be introduced to the loan officer, since possibly in the future you will need loan services also. An introduction made by the bank president to the loan officer will definitely work to your benifit when your need for a loan arises.

The whole trick here is to appear *very confident and self-assured.* Obviously, you don't have to use this precise wording. For variation you could say that you are the executor of your dead aunt's estate, and as soon as it's out of probate you'll have a substantial amount to invest. If you don't like that one, try saying that you are the union representative at your plant, and the union is looking for a small bank in which to deposit all of its retirement funds, etc. If things work out for you in establishing your personal accounts, you *can almost guarantee* the bank major deposits in the near future.

What should be the main point throughout this entire scenario is the undeniable fact that you are someone to reckon with. More importantly, once that "fact" is made clear, always keep the carrot out of the president's reach. Those large funds you spoke about will always be just out of the bank's reach if you play your cards right. In the meantime, your banker will fall all over trying to please you. This charade can last indefinitely, because after a short period of time the reputation you have established will far outshadow the reality of your personal finances. The banker will eventually forget your initial promises, because the banker will be out drinking his lunch or playing golf, while the staff still thinks of you as a "big shot." Mission accomplished. You now own your own bank!

PART III

15

BANK INVESTMENTS

One of the most difficult areas in which to offer advice is that of investments. This is not because the subject itself is complicated but because the majority of individuals seeking such advice haven't the vaguest idea of what they are trying to accomplish through an investment program. I can emphatically say that you should try to achieve the highest rate of interest available on every penny you have on deposit with a bank. However, you must maintain flexibility, or the result will negate the original investment. During my banking career I have seen many people invest in a bank instrument of deposit only to find that they needed the money and lost their interest because of an early withdrawal. This calamity can be avoided if you have even the most elementary plan to make the most of your investments. I won't go into the numerous investments that have a much greater return and higher risk factor, since these types of investments are too sophisticated for the average family. High-risk investments are generally left to those affluent enough to maintain a substantial sum of money for investment purposes, referred to as "risk capital." These people don't need my advice, and you don't either, at least not on the subject of risky investments. If you were aware of all the possibilities at your financial disposal, you might be tempted to invest your entire future.

The average family won't get rich using a bank's investment program. Based on net return, these are among the worst investments you can make. The *only* thing they have to offer is a degree of safety. Even though you will not become rich, you can at least increase your return on money you're probably not aware can earn money for you at all. In addition, I will show how certain bank investment opportunities that appear equal differ greatly in net return. This is outright deception on the bank's part, and you should be informed of the pitfalls that can cause you a substantial loss.

The first thing is to convince you that you *must* save some money out of each paycheck. Even the smallest amount will add up over a long period of time. Twenty-five dollars per week at a rate of only 5 percent would escalate in twenty years to $43,562.73, and these computations are based on an interest rate far below that which we could obtain. The point here is that you can garner large rewards with small investments as long as you continue to meet your savings objectives weekly.

NOW ACCOUNTS

Now that we have laid the simplest of ground rules, the next thing you *must* do is make use of every penny at your disposal. This holds even if you have use of the funds for only two or three days. This was not possible until recently, because the banking lobby in Washington worked long and hard persuading Congress to continue the law prohibiting the payment of interest on demand deposits (funds in your checking account). Now that this has changed we can use the flexibility to earn as much as possible with very little effort. If you haven't changed your checking account to a NOW account, do so as soon as possible. This is the only way you can collect interest at the current rate of 5.25 percent. Granted, this interest rate is ridiculous in these times of extreme inflation. But it is certainly better than no interest at all, which is what you previously received on checking account deposits.

The key to your NOW account is the *method of computation* of interest and whatever associated service charges are tacked on to the account. Since almost all NOW accounts pay 5.25 percent, you would think it wouldn't make any difference at which bank you opened your account. This is not the case, since the method of computing interest may vary substantially among institutions. This does not even take into consideration the dissimilarities of associated service charges. Some banks pay interest on the average *collected* balance for the month, while others pay interest on the average balance for the period. Some banks have a minimum balance requirement of as much as $1,000.00 before they will pay any interest. If your balance drops below $1,000.00 even for one day during the month, you lose all your interest for that period. Other banks have no minimum balance requirement. There are other methods of interest computation, but it is not necessary to review each one as long as the point has been made that all NOW accounts are not the same. You must shop around to find the most acceptable service.

Now we get to the service charges. Some banks charge a cost per check written, in most cases $.05, which is added to a basic monthly maintenance charge of $5.00 (sometimes more). These charges are subtracted from the interest earned, and the result is the net interest paid on your account. Again, there are numerous methods of computing these service charges.

Let's go right to the bottom line. What is the best NOW account you can secure? First, make sure the interest is computed on the *average daily balance* and not the average collected balance, which will be less. Next, you want a service charge that is either based on a use charge (for example, $.05 per check), or is a small monthly charge equivalent to (or less than) a charge if computed on the average number of checks you write each month. Stated another way, if you typically use fifty checks per month you should be looking for a service charge of approximately $2.50 per month. The bank, in this case, would break even on your account and still maintain its spread on your money. This spread is the bank's daily investment rate minus the 5.25 percent paid to you as interest. To illustrate how a difference in the method of computation of interest and charges can drastically alter your net interest, let's use an example of an account that uses fifty checks per month and has an average balance of $750.00, of which $300.00 is collected. Bank A has a minimum balance of $500.00, charges $.05 per check, and has a monthly service charge of $5.00. Bank A pays interest on the collected average balance. Bank B has a service charge of $2.00 per month, $.02 per check, and pays interest on the average balance, with no minimum balance requirement.

Bank A
Interest earned by customer

($300.00 × 5.25% divided by 12)	$ 1.31
Service charge	(5.00)
Use charge (50 × $.05)	(2.50)
Net profit (loss) to customer	($ 6.19)

Bank B
Interest earned by customer

($750.00 × 5.25% divided by 12)	$ 3.28
Service charge	(2.00)
Use charge (50 × $.02)	(1.00)
Net profit (loss) to customer	$ .28

Please note that in both cases the bank would have earned, in addition to the actual charges for the checking account, $8.12 at current rates of daily returns. This presents us with some interesting statistics. Bank A earns a total of $14.31 on your account, $6.19 of which came out of your pocket. Bank B earns a total of $7.84 even after paying you $.28 interest. Although all this may not seem too exciting, you should realize two important facts: (1) All bank accounts that appear equal are not, and (2) it pays to shop around. Finally, Bank B in our example is paying you only $.28 per month, which hardly qualifies as a good return. That is only a portion of the gain to you, as your net is really what you would have paid, and now have saved, added to the actual interest earned of $.28. These added together ($.28 + $6.19) equal $6.47. This computes to a yearly savings of $77.64, which I believe validates the need for some comparison shopping. It is well worth the effort. This service comparison, by the way, will not be easy. Most new accounts personnel at banks, and even a good many bank officers, are not well versed in explaining how interest and service charges are computed. Sometimes the bank seems to be keeping its method of computation secret even from its own staff. In any case, be persistent and you'll get the facts.

CLUB ACCOUNTS

Many banks are now offering CLUB accounts, which are simply checking accounts that, for a fee, offer free cashier's checks, money orders, an insurance policy, and free checks in addition to the standard checking account service. Although these seem to be quite fair, the actual monthly cost is extremely high, and the accounts are really just another way to feed the bank's coffers. The bank can well afford to provide these additional services, since the cost to the bank is small. Most of these CLUB accounts charge $3.00 to $5.00 per month, which is $36.00 to $60.00 per year. For these fees you would receive approximately $3.20 worth of checks, $5.00 worth of cashier's checks, and $10,000.00 worth of *accidental* life insurance (on which the bank actually makes money with no risk since they are the agent and not the insurer). In addition, you may be entitled to access to the bank's automatic teller. This packaging gimmick is designed to appeal to the uninformed consumer. Banks have managed to convince the public that a group of services purchased together are worth more than if purchased separately on an "as needed" basis. *Never* buy a CLUB account from your bank.

Let's take a good look at the area of actual savings. The most obvious place to start is with the regular passbook account. Unless absolutely necessary, never use a regular savings account. With the advent of the NOW account and the many types of certificates of deposit, there is no reason to place your money in an account that pays such low interest rates. This is especially true since banks, through their method of interest computation, reduce your paltry return even more. If you must have a regular savings account, look for a bank that pays interest from the day of deposit to the day of withdrawal, paying interest on a *daily* basis. Many banks use a *FIFO* or *LIFO* method of computing interest, which greatly reduces their expense. In addition, many banks pay interest only on those funds kept on deposit for the entire quarter, meaning that all deposit and withdrawal amounts during the period receive no interest at all. I'm not going to elaborate too much on this point, because there are so many different methods of computing interest. The important thing is to remember this and place your money only in the account recommended.

TIME CERTIFICATES OF DEPOSIT

Regular savings accounts have another serious drawback: The interest rate is so low that it doesn't even come close to breaking even with the current rate of inflation. After subtracting the necessary taxes, you may wonder why you started saving in the first place. More advantageous are a variety of new time certificates of deposit that at least pay a respectable return. The certificates still allow flexibility in your budgetary needs. When investing in TCD's, it is most important to realize that the key to making the best choice *is the rate of interest weighted against your need for use of the money*. Although some TCD's pay a higher rate of return, you must allow the bank use of your money for a longer time. During this time, which may be several years, you may find that you need the funds. When a withdrawal is made before the maturity date, a substantial interest penalty must be paid. Another possibility is the increase in the interest rate during the time period for the particular type of TCD you have. You are then earning less than you could. You should invest in a certificate that has the highest rate of return for the shortest period of time. For obvious reasons you would be much happier with a thirty-day TCD paying 9.5 percent than with a one-year TCD paying 11 percent. A 1.5 percent extra return in exchange for relinquishing access to your funds for an additional eleven months is not a very good bargain. On a $5,000 investment, and allowing for the time differential, you would be earning an additional $75 in return for your funds. Flexibility of funds is worth far more than $75. There are, of course, times when taking the longer-term investment makes sense. For example, not too long ago, TCD rates had risen to highs of 16 and 17 percent. At that point I was advising investors to take the long-term investment, because the rates would surely tumble downward, as they quickly did. This advice was valid only for those who had investment capital available, as opposed to those who simply wanted some return on money needed in the near future.

If you have a large amount of cash—say, $10,000—remember this small trick: Most TCD's have a minimum investment of $1,000. Instruct your bank to issue you 10 TCD's at $1,000 each. Consequently, if you need a portion of the money, you will be faced with an early withdrawal penalty only for whatever portion of the funds are needed. The remaining investment remains intact and will continue to earn the original interest rate. Banks do not encourage customers to use this strategy, since it involves ten times the servicing and time costs. Know what you want when you go into the bank, and don't settle for less just to make a banker's job easier. It's *your money*!

Remember that the specific advice I've offered here is dated material—what is sound advice today may be less reliable a week from now. The important thing is that you establish your investment goals, make use of *all* the money at your disposal, and always weigh the expected return against your ability to control your money.

INDIVIDUAL RETIREMENT ACCOUNTS

Although IRA's are not considered the norm in investments, they are being used by many families in anticipation of retirement. The concept of preparing for your own retirement independently is most admirable and astute. It is admirable because you feel it is your responsibility to plan financially for your future, and it is astute to realize that the Social Security system may be going bankrupt. If this occurs, there's no guarantee Social Security will be around when we need it. Although I applaud your preplanning for retirement, an IRA is a poor investment by any standards. It's only true worth is the net effect on your taxes. The actual return is quite a bit less. The government has allowed banks to quote the net result of an IRA in an attempt to entice investors. The government and banking communities hope that people will buy the package. In my opinion, the government knows that Social Security, as we know it today, cannot exist much longer. Consequently, your banker will quote you some interesting net returns that are not valid in terms of actual dollars. Considering the small actual return on IRA's, you may be much better off investing in other instruments that historically have returned more than the inflated IRA return rate. You eventually must pay taxes on an IRA, a fact that is conveniently ignored by your banker. Moreover, should you need the money earlier than your retirement date, the penalty is extremely severe. This penalty, together with the inflationary loss, probably will cause you to lose money. Again, there are other investment options that may, over the long run, return much more than you could have hoped for using an IRA. For this you need additional advice from a reputable professional. The primary purpose of this book is to make it easier for you to make intelligent decisions in dealing with your bank, not to entice you into other forms of investments.

16

THE INVESTMENT POOL

The small investor who tries to take advantage of certain bank investments that return the highest interest rate is often stymied. The minimum deposit requirement may force you to accept a low return. The bank does this for a specific reason. It wants to diminish paperwork, which adds substantially to the cost of money. Since banks are permitted, in many cases, to set their own allowable minimum for a particular investment, I won't attempt to outline all the possibilities. You have, no doubt, seen ads in newspapers, or in the bank lobby, for a 2½-year time certificate of deposit at 14 percent, minimum deposit $1,000. Other investments may require $5,000. Investments over $100,000 have an interest rate that is negotiable with the bank, and often this is the highest rate the bank will pay depositors. Of course, the obvious problem is that not many of us have $100,000 (or even $5,000, for that matter) to put into a savings certificate.

Since a bank can offer rates that are more advantageous to some individuals than to others, why not change the rules and get the most from your money? Contact your friends or relatives, and each take out a share of an investment pool that can then be deposited in an amount that will get you the higher rate. If an investment takes $10,000, convince five relatives to invest jointly $2,000 each, and deposit the money in an account with a title that protects each of you. Banks don't like this, because it takes extra time for the new-accounts staff to prepare the certificate. Furthermore, the bank stands a higher risk of making an error when the instrument is cashed in, since there are more people involved. But that's the bank's problem, not yours. Basically, the account name should read Mr. John Jones AND Mr. Jack Sizemore AND etc. The account title should represent *all* signatures required for withdrawal. It amazes me that more people don't take advantage of money pooling. In many cases, the interest rate can jump to the point of almost doubling. Banks, if they are really there to serve the community, should accept all investment deposits that satisfy the customers' wishes, provided all other requirements are met. You *can* beat interest discrimination by pooling your monies and investing as a group rather than as an individual.

When pooling money and thereby receiving a higher return on your investment, why not take this benefit to an even greater length? Most banks pay interest quarterly, even though the instrument may compound interest daily. This, of course, means the bank retains your money (interest) and can use that money until the time it is actually paid. Notice, if you have a loan outstanding, the bank eagerly wants to receive payments monthly, but when it comes to your interest, they prefer to keep it as long as possible. Depending on how the bank computes interest, it may be beneficial for you to request monthly payment of your interest. (Most banks will comply if asked.) The actual increase is relatively small, but I believe it is worth the extra effort. All you have to do is set up the program correctly in the first place and then forge ahead with it. Let's look at a simple example to illustrate my point further. A twelve-month time certificate of deposit today pays 9.8 percent at one bank I know and has a $10,000.00 minimum deposit. The current passbook rate is 5.25 percent. If five people invested $2,000.00 in a regular savings account that computed interest quarterly, their individual return in one year would be $2,107.08 ($107.08 interest). If they pooled their money and invested in the one $10,000.00 TCD, their net return each would be $2,203.32 ($203.32 interest). The difference in the net return is $96.24 per person. This is a net increase of 89.87 percent simply by pooling their money and by creating benefits generally reserved for more affluent investors.

If you had requested monthly payment of interest for the TCD instead of customary quarterly payment offered by the bank, your net return each would jump to $2,205.04. As I mentioned, the increase in this situation is minimal, but why allow the bank to have any of your money when it's not necessary? The additional $1.72 is an increase of only .84 percent to you personally, but if you apply that figure to a bank that maybe has $100 million in this type of time certificate, you would see that the bank has saved itself $840,000.00 in interest expense in a year! When you are dealing in hundreds of millions of dollars, .5 percent is a substantial sum of money. I would have no objection to the bank making the most of every investment opportunity at the customer's expense *if* they played by the same set of rules when lending you money. When you purchase a bank investment you are lending the bank money, and yet the bank is still setting all the rules in the same way as when you borrow money. The fair solution to this disparity rests with the appropriate governmental agencies ensuring that banks apply the same set of rules *whether they are the borrower or the lender.* You may wonder how the inequity continues to exist, and why the public tolerates it. But remember, the banking lobby is so strong in this country that changes are not to be anticipated in the foreseeable future. The only thing you can do now, though, is try to make the most from the bank and not settle for anything less than what you want. In most cases, banks have certain policies that will work in your favor, but the staff is instructed not to mention these conditions unless the customer asks. Monthly payment of interest is one of those conditions. Pooling several individuals' money to meet a minimum deposit requirement is another.

By the way, you should not be surprised by the concept of money pooling. That is exactly what you are doing when you invest in a mutual fund, and these have existed for years. In this case you are going to start your own mutual fund, except yours is going to be insured by the FDIC!

To be safe completely in this investment pool, have a written agreement with *all* the depositing parties if there is a problem in the future. This need not be a complicated document for it to be legal. Simply state in the body of the contract the intentions of all the parties. This may include eventualities, such as the rights of heirs should one party pass away, the inability to draw funds before maturity, the fact that the certificate cannot be used for borrowing by one party, etc. Make up your own agreement and have each party sign it, each receiving a copy for his or her files.

PART IV

PART IV

17

GAMES FOR FUN AND PROFIT

There are many ways to "get even" with your bank, and there are many ways to defraud it also. I could, for example, explain how you could completely ruin the bank's automated teller machine in less than five seconds, how effectively to close the bank's main vault for weeks, how to pass bad checks, how to fast-change a teller, how to ruin the bank's night depository in less than thirty seconds, etc. It's not that I'm devious. Rather, I've had a number of years of banking experience, and after being in that environment for so long I've seen almost everything one could imagine. I won't go into the various methods of literally destroying your bank because that type of activity is unnecessarily destructive and most definitely against the law. Some of these techniques are quite comical and inventive, but they do not represent what a sane, moral person would consider doing to express displeasure with a bank. There are, however, a number of perfectly legal ways to make the bank pay for its insensitive and sometimes unprofessional manner of doing business.

The principal and most effective way to accomplish this is to know the banking laws better than they do—and it won't be hard. I'll mention only a few ways to make my point. You can learn others by purchasing a copy of the appropriate banking manual that describes the specific banking laws as they relate to a state or nationally chartered bank. The Comptroller of the Currency manual applying to national banks can be purchased from the U.S. Governmental Printing Office in Washington, D.C. The state banking manual can be purchased from the office of the state banking commissioner in a particular state, or ordered from the FDIC office in Washington, D.C.

The main point to bear in mind is that most bank personnel can't possibly keep abreast of all the appropriate banking laws. There are too many of them. Banks don't spend much time worrying about this, because the regulatory agencies involved are extremely lax in enforcement. At any rate, with a little investigation you can find opportunities to create a chamber of horror for your bank. Believe it or not, in some cases you can actually receive compensation for the bank's errors!

For example, did you know that if you apply for a real-estate loan (that means actually applying, not just casually inquiring) the bank is obligated, at the time of your application, to provide you with a booklet, approved by the federal government, explaining certain aspects of a real-estate transaction? In addition, banks are required to present you with a good-faith estimate of the settlement charges you will incur during your real-estate closing. By law this must be in your possession twelve days before the closing of the loan. If this is not done, the bank can be liable for not supplying you the mandated information. If this were to be pursued in court, you could claim a sum for damages sustained due to the bank's neglect or $500, whichever is *greater*. Complete specifics relating to real-estate applications and closings are outlined in the Real Estate Settlement Procedures Act, which can be purchased through the U.S. Government Printing Office. Phone inquiries on the subject should be directed to HUD (the Department of Housing and Urban Development) in Washington, D.C. This is just one simple case where the bank can be held monetarily liable for not being professional and responsible. My experience has been that larger banks with sophisticated real-estate departments rarely make an error in this area. Smaller banks, conversely, rarely have a real-estate application and closing where an error doesn't occur. Some of these errors could make the customer a quick $500 if he or she is equipped with enough knowledge.

National banks are required to make available, upon request, a copy of certain financial information as specified under the Home Mortgage Disclosure Act of 1975. This information is very precise and, as the designation implies, refers to home mortgages only. A copy of the act is included in the comptroller of the currency manual. Basically the bank must show how comprehensively it is serving the community in providing home mortgages. All banks maintaining assets of $10 million or more for two consecutive years are obligated under this act. Surprisingly, even though banks are required to report this information to federal regulatory agencies, quite often banks are completely unprepared for a request for this information from a customer. To make matters even worse, a bank not in compliance may simply refuse the customer's request, or tell him or her to come back at a later date. This may occur even though the bank is legally obligated to have the information readily available. If you file a complaint with the appropriate agency against a bank in violation of this act, the bank will have to respond, explaining the circumstances. If the explanation does not satisfy the regulatory agency, the bank may be served with a cease-and-desist order. Further noncompliance could lead to the removal of an officer or director and possibly a fine. So you didn't make any money here, but maybe you've made your bank sit up and take notice. Or maybe you've paid them back for that check they erroneously sent back on your account!

If you are a shareholder in a nationally chartered bank, you can request to see the complete list of shareholders at any time the bank is open. You'd be amazed at what a commotion this can cause. Half of the bank's officers run around frantically trying to find out if you can do this, or where the list is kept. This is always good for a laugh, even when they are able to comply. The bank officials assume that you are copying certain names off the list for a devious reason. They immediately reason that a proxy fight is at hand, especially if the annual shareholders' meeting is near. If they don't comply with your request to see the list of shareholders, you should file a complaint with the comptroller of the currency if it is a national bank or the FDIC and state banking agency if it's a state-chartered bank. The bank will then have to go through the trouble of responding, and then admit their error to you. If you never give a reason for your request, which you are not obligated to do, the least you will accomplish is keeping your banker awake for a few nights wondering what is going on!

Under the Equal Credit Opportunity Act (15 U.S.C. 1691), banks have legal obligations to consumers, which sometimes cost them a great deal of money. The problem here is that the consumer is usually uninformed of the bank's responsibility. The act states that "it shall be unlawful for any creditor to discriminate against any applicant, with respect to any aspect of a credit transaction (1) on the basis of race, color, religion, national origin, sex or marital status, or age. . . ." This is the core of the act, and my experience has led me to believe that the intent of the act is violated almost every day in almost every bank. This results not because the bank, as an entity, is prejudiced against anyone in particular, or any specific group. The cause, as I see it, lies with the loan officers themselves. They are people, and that means they are guilty of certain personal prejudices that they cannot separate from their work. Women form one group that is regularly discriminated against. Loan officers, even though this is not permissible, will bring up at committee meetings a concern regarding pregnancy. How can she pay the loan back if she loses her job because she has to stay home to take care of the kid? Since refusing a loan is, in many cases, a completely subjective process, the loan officer conveniently finds another "reason" for the refusal, which is then entered on the rejection notice. This happens all the time. Young people are victims of a bank's prejudices. Banks feel that the credit worthiness of young people is unproven, and they prefer not to be the pacesetters in granting credit to them. All this indicates that banks violate the antidiscrimination laws regularly and are rarely called to task for their unprofessional and inequitable policies.

If you feel that you have been discriminated against, file a complaint to the appropriate government agency having jurisdiction over the particular bank. If you do not receive satisfaction, you may want to retain an attorney who will work on a percentage basis if you win your case. It is not difficult to find a lawyer who will represent you based on this fee arrangement, especially if you have even a remote chance of winning.

What can you win in this type of case? Civil liability allows that in addition to any actual damages you sustain due to discrimination, you can collect punitive damages of up to $10,000. If you file a class-action suit, the recovery cannot exceed the lesser of $500,000 or 1 percent of the net worth of the creditor. This doesn't necessarily mean that you will win if you file such a suit, but it does mean that there are weapons an individual can use against a bank. The bank doesn't want *bad* publicity, and sometimes even just the threat of a suit will encourage a banker to approve your loan application.

At other times the bank will roll over and play dead when faced with a customer who threatens to sue pursuant to the Equal Credit Opportunity Act because the bank knows that even if they win they will lose, at least from a monetary standpoint. If you have acquired legal representation from either an attorney or a Legal Aid group, the bank knows it may cost $50,000.00 worth of legal expenses on their part just to prove they are "clean." Quite often a bank suddenly realizes that it might be cheaper to take a risk on your loan than it would be to take a chance with a jury who might side with an individual against a faceless financial institution. In general, banks have good lawyers simply because they can afford to pay them. However, juries tend to favor an individual, assuming, of course, that you have a concrete reason to bring the case to court in the first place. It is unfortunate that more consumers don't bring suits against banks. The system will never change until it becomes too costly for a bank to continue to provide unfair service.

Under the Consumer Credit Protection Act (15 U.S.C. 1601–10), all banks are responsible for certain technical requirements when making a loan to an individual. These technicalities (laws, statutes, regulations, and interpretive rulings) are complicated and specific. Perhaps as many as one loan in twenty has an error in the presentation, meaning that the bank is in violation of the act. Again, the customer very rarely has enough information to be aware of the error. The bank, when the error is recognized, is certainly not going to mention it. Even when the examiners, in their general loan review, come across an error, they do little to the bank except note the error on the exam report. It's not their obligation to report the error to the injured party (the customer). Depending on the magnitude of the error, the customer may have many legal options, with monetary benefit as a possible end result. It would be an overwhelming task to discuss all the ramifications of this subject. But to summarize, when you receive the loan papers after signing them, check all the addition, multiply your payments by the number of months of the loan, and determine if the total equals the amount owed the bank. Be certain that the annual percentage rate is not misstated. If you find an error, go back to the bank. *Do not release your copy of the loan papers.* Ask your banker what is going to be done about the error and what legal avenues are open to you because of the mistake. This usually gets a good deal of attention. At this point, many compromises can be made that may very well be to your benefit. If you are still not satisfied, write to the appropriate government agency as mentioned earlier. You've got nothing to lose.

There are many options open to bank customers when an error is made by a bank. The remedies can sometimes be most profitable. I have mentioned just a few here to show you that you can fight back. Banks must be shown through monetary loss, or a threat of monetary loss, that responsibility to the community cannot be taken lightly. Bankers would counter this with the argument that the industry is overly regulated. What they neglect to mention is that the regulations are seldom if ever enforced. Therein lies the problem. Only the informed and assertive consumer can change this sad state of affairs.

18

YOUR RIGHTS AS A CONSUMER

Banks and other financial institutions are among the most highly regulated industries in the country, and you would think that your individual rights are most secure if you experience a problem. Nothing could be farther from the truth. Banks have more regulations than they have customers and are governed by numerous agencies such as state banking commissions, the Comptroller of the Currency, and the Federal Deposit Insurance Corporation. The problem is not the number of governing agencies nor the enormous number of regulations and banking laws but that the agencies, if at all possible, will avoid enforcing regulations.

State banking agencies (governing all state-chartered banks) are the worst of the lot. They are both ill equipped and understaffed to perform even the most superficial of exams and enforcement of consumer rights. The FDIC, while more sophisticated, relies on others in many cases to supply them with exam results and will almost always pass the problem on to the state agency, or the Comptroller of the Currency. The FDIC is the agency that all banks use in their advertising to make you feel at ease about your money. You know, "all deposits are insured up to $100,000." The fallacy is that while the FDIC has been successful during its existence, and has paid back depositors that had money in banks that closed, it is totally unprepared for a national banking catastrophe. As individual banks fold, the FDIC can cover the losses to customers, but they have in reserve only a small portion of the total deposits of FDIC-insured banks. Should the economy cause a truly serious disruption of the banking system, your FDIC insurance would be absolutely worthless.

The comptroller of the currency is another matter entirely. The comptroller's office governs all nationally chartered banks. (These banks have the word "national" included in their names.) The comptroller's office exemplifies the overall mismanagement of banks in general. In the recent past (it may be worse now), a regional administrator's office for a national bank region was well over a year behind in their exams of the national banks that fell under their jurisdiction. There was one person answering consumer complaints in an office, I was told, that received hundreds of complaints weekly. Try calling this office to speak with a specific individual on a Friday, and the odds are overwhelming that the party will not be there. Friday is a swing day, and the majority of the staff is off. How can they be so far behind and still allow the staff to operate on a four-day workweek? Is it any wonder they are behind in processing work?

Examiners who came into our bank would typically start their exam Monday morning at about 11:00 A.M. They would leave at 4:30 P.M., or before, each day. They would work only a half day on Wednesday and only a maximum of a half day on Friday. (The exam would last only a week.) A banking office cannot properly and comprehensively be examined in such a short time. Even sadder is that a good portion of the working time of the examiners was spent in attempts to enlist the help of a bank officer in securing employment at that particular bank. Examiners seem to fall in one of three categories. They have held their job so long they are only concerned with their retirement benefits and how much longer they will have to work, or they are brand-new examiners just out of college, or they are actively looking for new employment.

I am not exaggerating. The massive problems with governmental assistance to the banking industry are suggested by the thirty financial institutions that have folded during the past ten months. As I write this book, our economy has gone through some very difficult times. These bank closings have not been matched since the Great Depression of the 1930s. When the economy is healthy, any bank, no matter how inept, can make enough money to cover all its mistakes. However, when economic conditions start getting rough, the absence of strict banking regulation causes banks to start falling like overripe apples in late fall. Governmental agencies help create and then perpetuate a situation where your deposits and financial well-being are at the mercy of your local bank.

This is easy to understand if you realize that governmental agencies have a primary purpose: to keep a bank open regardless of whether your deposits are in safe banks. These agencies continue to function despite the number of bank closings or bank scandals. I believe that as many as 30 percent of all banks in this country are ready to fold, or should be closed. But the Administrator of National Banks, the FDIC, and local state agencies cannot afford to have that happen. These regulatory authorities will do unbelievable things to prevent failure even of banks that have no right to be in business.

Once a smart banker realizes that the agencies are nothing more than paper tigers, he is in a position to virtually steal his bank blind, either literally or by running up bills at the shareholders' expense. This brings us to an important point in this chapter: *Never* purchase more than a few shares of bank stock as investment. (A few shares are good, since you will receive special treatment reserved for "family.") Even though you are a shareholder you will never receive enough information from the bank to realize that the board of directors, the bank staff, and indirectly the appropriate governmental agency are all doing their utmost to fleece you. Bankers often make an additional 30 percent of their salary in benefits that are never reflected in the banks' statements. The board of directors, a local group elected by the shareholders and approved by the government, bear the ultimate responsibility for the day-to-day operation of the bank, yet they are often ill equipped to understand the information presented to them by bank management. Board members serve for two reasons primarily. First, they have gigantic egos and like to be recognized as community leaders with clout, and second, they have every intention of making money through their association with the bank. In terms of hands-on supervision they have nothing to offer, and more often than not, they hinder the overall effectiveness of the bank. Why, then, have a local board of directors? I believe that governmental agencies have planned this banking hierarchy to mask their inability to administer guidance properly.

If the general population knew to what extremes the governmental agencies will go to protect the system (while letting the consumer's needs be exploited and abused), the country would probably face a run on the banks that would make that of the Great Depression look like a small inconvenience. During my banking career I saw a number of embezzlements that altogether totaled close to $500,000. Five different people were involved in five different banks. How many of these individuals went to jail? How many of the embezzlements became public knowledge? None. The bank and the governmental agencies were more interested in maintaining an image of a bank's financial security than enforcing the law. Most bank officers are well aware they are in a position to steal, and even if caught, they stand a very good chance of walking off unscathed. I know of a case where the second officer in a bank was caught molesting a child. The bank interceded, took care of appeasing the police and the family of the young girl, and paid for the offender and his family to relocate to another state. The incident never made any of the papers. The point in mentioning this terribly sad and scandalous incident is to illustrate emphatically that the entire system is designed to protect the bank and its image. This concern with image comes first—before shareholders' investments, depositors' money, and the wellbeing of the community.

How does this situation affect you? During the course of your banking relationship I hope you never experience a problem so difficult that you cannot arrive at an equitable solution with the bank. However, should this occur, ignore all avenues that are cosmetically designed to create the appearance of governmental interest or assistance. National banks have placed in the lobby booklets entitled "Do You Have a Consumer Complaint?" If you read the material you may conclude that the comptroller's office is ready and eager to respond to your case and champion your interest. Not so. After I left banking, I personally filed a complaint as a private citizen regarding a national bank involving a check for $5,200. The specific details of the altercation are not relevant here except to say we had a difference of opinion that could not be settled amicably. In March 1982, I wrote the regional administrator's office, Comptroller of the Currency, and filed my complaint. I never received a reply to the first letter. I wrote other letters and placed numerous phone calls in an attempt to receive action. It was not until mid-September that I finally received a notice that my complaint had been received. This response came after I had mailed eight pieces of correspondence. Finally, six months following my initial complaint, the regional administrator's office wrote that they could not intervene, since I had filed litigation in an attempt to reclaim the money I felt rightfully belonged to me. What these officials failed to notice was that the reason for litigation in the first place was their own failure in carrying out regulatory responsibility and supervision. The case will be coming up soon, and the court will review the facts and decide on the distribution of the check. Governmental agencies will do whatever is necessary to protect a bank, and allow the consumer to bear the brunt of the system's ineptness.

If you have a problem with a financial institution, write *one* letter to the appropriate agency, and after waiting a reasonable length of time for a response, contact a lawyer. If you can't afford legal advice, or if the amount involved is less than an attorney's fee for taking the case, write your local newspaper's Action Line (or whatever it is called in your area). This is an excellent approach, because banks hate bad publicity. They will usually respond quickly when it is apparent that you will use whatever legal means are at your disposal to right a wrong to you. The bank has a distinct advantage, since it has the protection of regulatory agencies, and a lot more money than you do to battle it out in court. But you have the bank's fear of bad publicity working on your side, and this is something intolerable to a bank's image. Assertiveness and the willingness to fight are your best weapons.

19

SMALL CLAIMS COURT: THE BANKER'S NIGHTMARE

No one hires a lawyer to take a bank to court over overdraft charges, a loan late charge, or an error in cashing a check—it costs too much. But you can take a bank to court without hiring a lawyer, and you can win your case. Small Claims Court is the place to do it, and if you have a reasonable cause of action (i.e., a case) you have a distinct advantage over the bank for the following reasons:

1. You will know the case better (it's yours) than anyone they can possibly send to represent the bank. In a higher court the bank's lawyer would be a distinct threat. In Small Claims Court the simplicity of case presentation and the absence of pomp work to your advantage. Some states do not even allow lawyers in Small Claims Court. If this is the case, it's just you against the banker.

2. Judges and most certainly juries have a lot more sympathy for one small person than for a million-dollar bank. Some states prohibit jury trials in Small Claims Court. The sympathy advantage you may have as "the small person" may tip the scales in your favor.

3. If the amount in dispute is small and your state does

not allow lawyers in Small Claims Court, your banker probably will not show up at all (in which case you would win by default). Perhaps the bank will agree to settle out of court and not be bothered further. Depending on the nature of your problem, you can drag the bank president, or some other high-ranking officer into court, costing him the entire day.

4. If your state does allow attorneys in Small Claims Court, a few hours of the attorney's time would cost the bank far more than the settlement.

5. Banks intensely dislike bad publicity. If a banker can buy his way out of a sticky situation he will, rather than go to court. Once a bank is served with a court order and realizes that you are serious, your odds of settling and receiving what you wanted in the first place are quite good.

6. You can subpoena all individuals relevant to the case. In certain situations you may be able to drag half the bank into court. It's obvious the bank can't afford this, especially if the case involves a small amount. To a bank, because of the settlement limitations of Small Claims Court, a suit filed here may not be considered worth fighting.

The primary purpose of Small Claims Court is to provide less affluent claimants with a small legal claim the opportunity for a fair decision. In general, Small Claims Court provides a procedure for claims not exceeding a certain amount, usually $500 to $1,500. Traditional court proceedings are not practiced here, and the case simply evolves into a general conversation, with the judge (sometimes called the referee) as mediator. The substance of your case, however, must adhere to the general principles of law. The court will not settle disputes that have no legal basis for a monetary award. Cases presented to Small Claims Court involving substantial legal presentations will often be referred to a regular court by the judge. The formal rules of evidence do not apply to Small Claims Court, and this is where *you have a distinct advantage over the bank*. Small Claims Court contends that if formal rules of evidence were followed here the reason for the court's existence would be negated. The vast majority of Small Claims Court cases are consumer-oriented, and the court realizes that the individual either did not receive, or retain, the evidence necessary for formal presentation. The advantage here is clearly yours. Your word and that of your witnesses may very well be more important than all the paperwork at the disposal of the bank.

Filing a Small Claims Court case is very inexpensive (usually less than $25), and should you win your case, the judge usually allows you to recover your filing fee. All you need do is state your case in everyday language. Cases come to trial quickly, without the long delay that other courts usually face. You relate your side of the case, and the bank responds. The decision is rendered either immediately or within a few days.

In preparing for your case, it will do well for you to visit your local library, or a law school library. You will need to do some research. There is always someone at the library to help you if you need assistance. Next, visit the court itself and talk to the court clerk, asking the following questions:

1. What are the monetary limitations of Small Claims Court in this state? (They vary from state to state.)
2. What are the court's jurisdiction limitations? (This is to determine whether you can sue in that court.)
3. What are the court's rules? (Many times they have a booklet that will give you quite a bit of information.)
4. What forms do I need to start a case?
5. What are the filing fees involved? Can they be recovered if I win my case?

Once you have this basic information, you can begin to process your case, putting the bank on notice (through service of a summons). It's not uncommon, after being served, that the bank will call you directly with a settlement offer. If the bank offers to settle out of court, get the offer in writing. You can then present the offer agreement to the court so it can be legally enforced.

If the case goes to court, briefly state your position, and present your evidence without taking more time than absolutely necessary. Don't make rash accusations about the bank, or specific bank officers. Your demeanor will be very important in the court's eyes. Since court schedules are tight, make the most of the time allowed you.

In your case against the bank, *preparation is the key to winning*. Gather all the pertinent receipts, bills, canceled checks, etc. Arrange for all your witnesses to be subpoenaed. They are needed to reinforce your position. Prepare yourself with notes, and organize all your documents.

If all of this seems too confusing, go to your local bookstore and purchase one of the many paperbacks that completely describe the Small Claims Court experience. To set your mind at ease, included here is an example of a typical form for a Small Claims Court claimant's statement. This is all you really need to get started. Following that, all you need are the time and dedication to pursue the matter to a just conclusion.

Basically, forms such as these are all you need to get the ball rolling and turn the tables on the bank.

Not only will the bank sit up and take notice when you file a claim, but also in all likelihood you will win your argument. Usually customers just close their accounts following a dispute—a technique that doesn't impress banks at all. After all, what are a few lost individual accounts? When you become responsible for forcing representatives from the bank to appear in court, their attitude changes dramatically.

I would like to close this chapter with a few important points that may determine the outcome of your case.

As human beings, judges can make mistakes, too. If you wish to appeal the decision (which you may have a right to do), go right ahead. (Note that in some Small Claims Courts, decisions rendered by a referee cannot be appealed.) Remember, if you want justice in your case against the bank, you must be willing to fight for it. In the same light, remember also that people like being treated with respect and courtesy. That includes the judge. There's no harm in trying to establish a friendly rapport with the judge in your quest for monetary justice.

Your attitude in a Small Claims Court case is most impor-

FORM 3. TYPICAL FORM FOR SMALL CLAIMS COURT CLAIMANT'S STATEMENT

STATE OF ILLINOIS

IN THE CIRCUIT COURT OF THE 19TH JUDICIAL CIRCUIT

McHENRY COUNTY

Complaint..   Case Number.......................

_____

_____   VS   _____

_____   _____

        Plaintiff(s)   **Defendant(s)**

SMALL CLAIM COMPLAINT

I, the undersigned, claim that the defendant is indebted to the plaintiff in the sum of $..for...

_____

_____

and that the plaintiff has demanded payment of said sum; that the defendant refused to pay the same and no part thereof has been paid; that the defendant resides at...

Phone No.................................: that the plaintiff resides at...

....Phone No...........................: in the State of Illinois.

Date..............................   _____
       (Month   Day   Year)   (Signature of Plaintiff)

AFFIDAVIT

....on oath states that the allegations in this complaint are true.

_____

Signed and sworn to before me...................................., 19.......

(SEAL)

_____
                (Notary Public)

FEES			Plaintiff..... in Court..........................
CLERK'S			Defendant..... in Court..........................
Certified Mail			Judgment for..........................
Sheriff			$.................................Costs $..........
Execution			Stay.........................days Date..........
			Against..........................
			....
			....
			Dismissed as to..........................
			....
			....
			....
			(Judge or Magistrate)

White-Court Copy; Pink-Defendant's Copy; Yellow-Plaintiff's Copy; Green-Copy

FORM 4. TYPICAL SUMMONS FORM FOR SMALL CLAIMS COURT

SUMMONS—Small Claims

IN THE CIRCUIT COURT OF THE NINETEENTH JUDICIAL CIRCUIT

McHENRY COUNTY, ILLINOIS

_____

Plaintiff(s)

vs.

No. _____

Amount Claimed _____

_____

Defendant(s)

SUMMONS

To each defendant:

YOU ARE SUMMONED and required to appear before this Court at Associate Division Court 2200 N. Seminary Avenue, Woodstock, Illinois, Room _____ at _____ o'clock___m., on _____ 19____ to answer the complaint in this case, a copy of which is hereto attached. **IF YOU FAIL TO DO SO, A JUDGMENT BY DEFAULT MAY BE TAKEN AGAINST YOU FOR THE RELIEF ASKED IN THE COMPLAINT.**

To the officer:

This summons must be returned by the officer or other person to whom it was given for service, with indorsement of service and fees, if any, immediately after service and not less than three days before the day for appearance. If service cannot be made, this summons shall be returned so indorsed. This summons may not be served later than three days before the day for appearance.

(Seal of Court)

Name

Attorney for

Address

City

Telephone

Witness _____ 19

_____
Clerk of Court

Date of Service _____ 19____
(To be inserted by officer on copy left with defendant or other person)

Insert date which is not less than 14 or more than 40 days after issuance.

NOTICE TO DEFENDANT

If you wish to contest this claim, you must do the following:

(a) File a written appearance (form may be obtained at the court) on or before the day specified above for your appearance, hereafter called the return day.

(b) If the complaint is verified (sworn to), your case will be tried on the 7th day after return day and you should be present in court at the above specified address prepared to go to trial.

(c) If the complaint is not verified, your case will be tried on the return day and you should be present in court at the above specified address prepared to go to trial.

(d) If you are not certain whether or not the complaint is verified, inquire of the clerk of the court.

If you do not wish to contest this claim, you need not appear in person or file a written appearance, and a judgment will be entered against you on the return day.

tant. You'll have to be both a courteous and an assertive consumer who feels he or she has been wronged. Use common sense in putting your best foot forward, both in appearance and demeanor. Be polite and follow the judge's orders, yet be assertive in your presentation. Assertive, courteous people are admirable foes.

The key to your legal hassle with the bank is the preparation you make before the case is heard in court. This preparation will be crucial to your success or failure. You are going to get one shot to present the circumstances of the case. If you walk into court unprepared, the judge is going to become annoyed because you are wasting the court's time. Furthermore, the opposition will try to make you feel like a fool. You might have the strongest case in the history of jurisprudence, but if you can't put the facts together in a cohesive presentation, you won't stand a chance of winning your case. Small Claims Court is the only court where the little guy is on equal footing with even the largest corporation. Don't waste the opportunity to balance the scales by being unprepared.

Dedication on your part in seeing that the bank does what it was supposed to do in the first place is important. Remember that judges hear many cases every day, and yours will not be as special to a judge as it is to you. *Dedication and preparation* will make you a winner.

Banks are big and powerful, and they know it. They use this knowledge to their advantage as they continually trample on consumers. A bank will do whatever it wishes, to whomever it wishes, as long as no one fights back. Like most bullies, they'll run scared when their actions are met with opposition. When, in your honest opinion, the bank has made an error, or taken advantage of you, *go after it.*

Banks abhor being served with a summons to appear in court. Bankers also hate being personally served the summons. My own opinion is that banks have this aversion to Small Claims Courts because they often know that the problem was their fault. The odds are that they will lose the case and be embarrassed in the process. If you're really angry with the bank, you might want to contact the local paper (especially if you are in a small town) before the trial, and without saying too much about the case, simply show them the court statements (which are public information), and let the newspaper decide if they want to cover it.

As powerful as banks are, in Small Claims Court they can be brought down to size and held accountable for their actions.

20

THE ART OF INTIMIDATION

How many times have you allowed yourself to be taken advantage of simply because you were afraid to make a scene? When it comes to your bank, you probably lost money while you were being intimidated. This inevitably occurs when a bad situation is allowed to exist, and you, the customer, are afraid to speak up or make a demand. Also, the complexity of most banking transactions doesn't hurt the bank's position as intimidator. Although the bank is very good at exploiting a situation such as this, it is ill equipped to handle a customer who turns the tables and becomes the aggressor.

You *do* have at your disposal the freedom to attack: You *can* cause a scene to alter a loan arrangement, recoup an unfair service charge, or get your due in any of a number of other ways. There are many reasons why people don't speak up to their bank. Perhaps it's not your nature to be aggressive, or you just don't understand the transaction. But whatever the reason, you can save yourself a lot of money by speaking up loudly and firmly. To be adept at turning the tables on your banker, you must display your mistrust or anger *before* the fact. By doing so, you cause the banker to prove to you that the bank is professional enough to warrant your trust and business. For instance, it is amazing that people will enter into a long-term mortgage (which ultimately costs a family hundreds of thousands of dollars) and yet be reluctant or afraid to speak up in an attempt to negotiate a better deal. The bank—and I can say this from personal career experience—relies on its ability to intimidate the customer. As a customer in any situation, you must anticipate the possibilities, then make the bank aware that you will settle for nothing less than the best deal for you.

Never be afraid to act on behalf of your financial future. Often in dealing with a bank this means being offensive, since the bank is familiar with doing things its own way. I think it is far better to be offensive than be taken advantage of. You just may have to call off a mortgage loan deal at the closing, or call the police if the bank improperly repossesses your car. However, these types of situations generally are repulsive to most people. Those who are inherently passive would find any of these situations hard to handle. We tend to ask the bank the interest rate on a new car loan and then accept it without further comment. We do this even though we know that in any business deal that involves money there is room for negotiation. We fail to realize that we *do* have alternatives. We can always take our business elsewhere. We can close our checking account (the bank's most profitable type of account), or our savings account. Within reason we can, by word of mouth, create negative advertising for the bank. You have something a bank wants: *money*. There is an old saying that "money talks." In short, there are numerous leverage threats that can be used against your bank. Unfortunately, most people are too shy or embarrassed to try them. Yet the bank isn't too shy or embarrassed to turn down your loan, repossess your car, or foreclose on your mortgage. The bank has the upper hand.

It makes sense, then, that you be extremely careful in dealing with the bank when there is a large sum of money at stake, such as a mortgage loan commitment. Making a federal case out of a $10 overdraft charge might not make the most sense. On the other hand, that doesn't mean you should passively let the bank bleed you to death. If you feel you have been wronged by the bank, no matter what the amount, consider taking action.

Many times there is the possibility of negotiation even when it appears that it is not possible. Today's high mortgage rates reinforce this point. We have already discussed mortgage lending, but what about the mortgage loan that has had twenty years elapse on a twenty-nine-year amortization? Many people are in a position when near retirement, or if they come into a large sum of money, to consider paying off their mortgage entirely. What should they do? Many people would pay off the total amount still owing. This mistake may cost them thousands of dollars. Older mortgages are usually at a rate so low that the bank is losing money in serving them since the bank's cost of money has gone up dramatically in the past few years. Consequently, many financial institutions have gone as far as offering mortgage customers a reduction in their entire mortgage if they agree to pay off the loan before it is due to mature. Other banks will make this concession to those customers who will take the time to make an offer. That's right: *You make an offer to the bank!* Let's put together an example to make this point. Consider a mortgage loan with a principal balance remaining of $15,000 for ten years, at 6 percent. Assuming you were able to pay off this loan, what are your options? First, you could immediately pay off the loan, handing the bank $15,000 in cash. Or you could invest the monies at the current interest rate of 13.5 percent (choice of best bank investment). This, of course, would mean that you could "make" an additional 7.5 percent on your money, but the term of your investment would only be for two and a half years. At that point you would be at the mercy of the current rate structure. It may be more, or it could be substantially less. There is a definite gamble here no matter how you look at it—unless you make the bank an offer it can't refuse. Remember that banks can make much more on their investments than you can on yours. While at present you can make an additional 7.5 percent on your investment (if you don't pay off the loan and invest the monies instead), the bank can invest the same money at 19.5 percent. This means that the bank is losing 13.5 percent on your mortgage loan every year. Without running an amortization schedule to show the loan's actual reduction, for the sake of simplicity let's say the loan is reduced one tenth per year. (This isn't the way it exactly works, but it does balance out to almost the same in actuality.) Let's see who earns more if you *don't* pay off the loan and invest the money instead.

Principal	Your Earnings	The Bank's Loss
$ 15,000	$ 1,125	$ 2,025
13,500	1,125	1,822
12,000	1,125	1,620
10,500	1,125	1,417
9,000	1,125	1,215
7,500	1,125	945
6,000	1,125	810
4,500	1,125	607
3,000	1,125	405
1,500	1,125	202
Totals	$ 11,250	$ 11,068

At this point it appears that there is no distinct advantage resulting from an offer made to the bank, at least from your end. Right? *Wrong.* First, this assumes that interest rates will remain constant. This assumption is necessary so we can make a valid comparison. It would appear that the bank is going to lose $11,068 on your mortgage over the next ten years. Of course, it doesn't actually lose anything, but it does lose the *opportunity* to make *more* money. Why not, armed with your own mortgage amortization schedule, offer to pay off the loan principal if the bank will split their "profit" with you? However, your suggested "split" will be 75 percent of "their" money simply because the money isn't theirs until you decide to pay off your loan. Right now they are stuck with your mortgage, and $2,767 (25 percent of $11,068) is better than nothing. This will be even more emphatic when you play your ace, which we will get to in a moment. Seventy-five percent (your cut) equals $8,300, which you can now invest for ten years. Now let's examine what this does to your proposition.

Interest Saved by Paying Off Loan	Interest Earned on $8,300
$ 900	$ 1,120
810	1,120
720	1,120
630	1,120
540	1,120
450	1,120
360	1,120
270	1,120
180	1,120
90	1,120
Totals $ 4,950	$ 11,200

By adding your savings to the actual interest earned, you made a total of $16,150, as opposed to the $11,200 you would have made by not paying off the loan. Those of you who are skeptical probably are saying that the bank wouldn't agree to this. It is now time for you to play your ace. If the bank will agree to your offer, you will guarantee them in writing that you will keep the $8,300 in their bank for the entire length of time that was remaining on your loan (ten years). This means that the bank will have $8,300 to invest for the ten years at a profit margin of 6 percent. The bank will earn an additional $4,980 during that period. This coupled with the 25 percent of the mortgage payoff gain ($2,767) means that the bank will earn a total of $7,747, while you make an additional $4,900 ($16,150 minus $11,250). Out of the total amount earned, $12,647 ($7,747 plus $4,900), the bank earned 61 percent. The 75 percent/25 percent split really turns out to be a 61 percent/39 percent split in the bank's favor. The specifics of your offer can be whatever you feel is fair, since this is merely an example. Regardless of how you put it together, if you can't sell this cooperative deal to your banker, you probably couldn't convince a person dying of thirst to drink water. Everyone makes out on this deal, so why wouldn't your bank make you an offer like this? A few banks are, but the bulk of the banking community is just too lazy to work out this type of arrangement. Bankers aren't overly imaginative, or they just wouldn't be able to understand the basic benefits here. That's why you have to approach your banker with the proper figures. My whole point is that in many cases *you* hold the cards (*money*) and should take advantage of the situation. In the process you can make a bundle.

In any dealings with your bank, you must ask all questions you may have regarding a specific transaction. Many of us are afraid of appearing foolish, or even cheap, by asking for a detailed description of all charges on a loan agreement. Strangely enough, many of these same people will travel ten miles out of their way to get the special at a supermarket, or three cents less on a gallon of gas. Yet with their bank they passively sit back while huge sums of money are eaten up right before their eyes. Your personal finances should be one of the most important considerations in the life of your family. Make your banker detail each item on that loan form, or specify the details on any other transaction. Demand information that will allow you to make an informed choice. If you don't like what you hear, go to another bank. They are as plentiful as gas stations. Demand to be treated with respect and consideration. Don't be afraid to ask for a receipt for monies paid to the bank for a loan payment, or even for a deposit. Remember, the more you demand from your bank, the more respect you will receive. Simply demand from the bank the same standard of conduct they demand from you. Your banker may not like you for this but will definitely respect you.

Never accept the bank's word for anything. Their figures can be wrong, too. The odds of the bank being correct are in their favor, judging from my experience, but they do make mistakes. A bank's computer is not infallible. Don't get ripped off just because the bank says you made an error. If they claim you're overdrawn and you know you're not, make them prove that they had just cause for the invasion of your checking account. One of the main reasons for your assertive attitude with the bank is that your account might have been used by others, either from inside the bank or outside. Since this is possible, you must not accept the bank's claim if you feel there is a possibility of an error not of your making. The bank's figures may be correct, but the input to your account may not if the bank has become the victim of fraud or embezzlement. Speaking up immediately can be the key to avoiding a long, drawn-out hassle in attempting to get your money back.

You've probably noticed that the bank, when you owe them money, gets everything in writing. They paperwork you to death, and every legal angle is covered. However, when you want something, your banker will make notes in his records and assure you not to worry because he'll remember the conversation and what was promised you. I have seen many couples buying a home get the short end of the stick at the bank. They go in seeking a mortgage commitment, or a loan for a car, and the banker tells them there's no problem, and he's sure the bank will be able to help. The couple shops around, and after making a deal on a car will go back to the bank only to find out that the banker can't lend that much money on that particular car, or the interest rate quoted was for a different term, or the bank's loan and discount committee has placed a freeze on this type of loan for a month, etc. Many times a customer will be given a verbal commitment from a banker on an extension for a loan, or an option to renew for an additional ninety or 180 days, only to discover when the time for the renewal arrives that the banker is no longer employed by the bank. If the banker is still there, he or she may say that the economy has changed and he or she can't help out right now, or the banker doesn't remember the original conversation. I've seen this happen time and again to bank customers. Their whole financial timetable has been ruined because they didn't have the banker put in writing the terms discussed orally. If the banker objects to putting his stated intentions in writing, go to another bank. The banker is not functioning in a professional manner and does not deserve your business.

Vow to change your attitude toward banks and bankers.

That alone will save you a great deal of time and aggravation at the bank. But what are you going to do if you really run into a brick wall with a banking problem? The ultimate answer here will be determined by your own conscience and personality. You will need to act in a manner you can live with and one that is in proportion to the problem at hand. You don't want to be unreasonable over petty issues that have little or no monetary value, and yet it does pay to let the bank know, whenever possible, that you are *the* customer, not just *a* customer. Respect is something we all deserve. It is not until we encourage someone to show us disrespect that we have a problem. Like many service corporations, banks have forgotten their obligations to service the community. I would like to give you three situations where bank customers retaliated successfully.

In each of the following cases the actions of the customer worked because of one fatal flaw in banks. Recently, a consumer banking survey determined that the primary concern of consumers regarding their bank was security. Banks have done as much as possible to enhance an image of security. Take a good look at the banking facility, the staff, the president, etc. In each case, the security image is of primary concern. Banks are very much concerned about their image, and they don't want it tarnished. When a customer challenges the security image, the bank in most cases becomes a helpless pawn that can be manipulated. The examples I'm going to give you are not to be used because I don't condone these methods, but I can't argue with their success, either.

An elderly woman had a bank loan with a remaining balance of approximately $600. The loan was secured by her furniture. She had been making her payments promptly for about two years when she ran into some problems with her Social Security payments. The payments ceased because of an unknown government technicality. For the first time in her life she could not pay her bills, and the bank loan was one of them. After she was about ninety days past due, the bank started pressing pretty hard on the woman to pay up or lose her furniture. She offered to make payments of $10 per month, but this was not acceptable to the bank. The loan officer was sympathetic, but the board of directors wanted this loan off the books immediately. The one particular board member who pushed hardest on this insignificant loan was a man worth millions of dollars. The loan officer told the board that he was not going to take the woman's furniture and he would rather write off the loan, since he knew the circumstances were beyond the customer's control. This argument continued for months within the bank until one day the insistent director came into the bank and ordered the loan officer to accompany him in visiting the woman. He was prepared to take the furniture if the past-due loan payments were not to be made up immediately. Two hours later the loan officer returned to the bank alone. He was somewhat shaken but laughing. When asked what had happened, he said that the bank was going to charge off the loan, and the issue was over once and for all. He further explained that the two of them had gone to the woman's house, and the director became extremely abusive to her, telling the woman that he was demanding immediate payment of the past-due amount. After much harassment the woman finally excused herself and went into another room. After a few minutes she returned carrying a pistol. She calmly sat down and told the director and loan officer not to move. She repeated the circumstances leading to the overdue payments and told the director that the bank had made her life miserable and she wasn't going to tolerate it any longer. The director's threats were the final straw. She explained that the bank had two choices: either leave her alone, or she would end all their lives right then and there. The director hastily wrote a note in a shaky hand stating that the bank obligation was paid off, and the woman would not be bothered again. This piece of paper was legally worthless, since it was made under duress. However, the bank never went near this customer again. What she did was obviously wrong. But the bank could have accepted her offer of $10 per month and eventually recouped the money. They had all the power, and that old woman was helpless. It was only when the bank officer and director experienced first hand what it felt like to think that their lives might soon be over that they understood the desperation the woman felt.

Again, she was wrong, and she could have killed someone, but in this case she won a small victory. She fought back in the only way she knew how. Like most bullies, when faced with force, the bank folded their tents and retreated.

Another case involves a young couple who received verbal approval from their bank for a car loan. They were planning to purchase from a local car dealership. Everything was in order. The application had been completed, and the credit check was acceptable. All that remained was for the couple to come to the bank to sign the papers. However, when they came to complete the paperwork, a major problem arose. The bank officer had prepared the check payable to both the couple *and* the car dealership, as is customary. After seeing the check, the husband told him a mistake had been made. The car was being purchased not from the local dealer but from another dealer from whom they had gotten a much better deal. It was the same model car, but they had saved hundreds of dollars. The bank officer told them that this changed the entire situation, and consequently he wouldn't be able to make the loan after all. The couple could not obtain an answer as to why this change in dealership made any difference. After a good deal of frustration, the husband became angry and ended up reaching over the desk and punching the loan officer in the nose. The couple then stormed out of the bank. What the couple didn't know was that their credit rating was marginal. Since the car was originally being purchased from the local dealer (who was also a bank director and major shareholder), the bank had overlooked the marginal credit rating. The loan was going to be made since "it was all in the family." This bank had been operating in a similar way for years and had made arrangements with the car dealer as well as with other local merchants who were also bank directors. This procedure succeeded in steering customers to their businesses using the availability of a loan as bait. The bottom line on this situation is that the bank had been a shill for local bank directors, but this time the loan officer was caught in the middle. The customers never knew the real reason for the rejection. The customers had kept their copy of the loan papers that had been signed, and the next day the husband came back to the bank and asked to see the president. The president was uneasy and called the police. When they arrived, the president, the customer, and the police met in the president's office. The president threatened to have the man arrested for assaulting the loan officer the preceding day. The customer related his side of the story (still not aware of the actual reason behind the problem), and the police suggested that the customer contact the Better Business Bureau as well as the state attorney's office. The policeman felt that the bank had entered into a valid contract and might have trouble explaining the rejection to the appropriate agencies. The bank president, apparently realizing that the bank now had a very real problem, asked the police to leave, telling them that something could be worked out. The customer, realizing this was to his advantage, sat and listened patiently to the president's offer. The bank would not press charges and would proceed to honor the loan commitment previously made. The customer explained to the president that his offer couldn't compensate for the aggravation he and his wife had been caused, not to mention the embarrassment of having to tell the car dealer that the loan had fallen through. The customer wanted the bank to initiate some action that would set things straight. He wanted more than the bank had originally offered. As far as the assault charges were concerned, he wasn't really worried because no one except his wife and the loan officer saw the incident. He knew it would be their word against the loan officer's. Contributing to his lack of concern about the assault was the fact that he felt completely justified in his actions due to the loan officer's attitude. However, there's no doubt he was wrong in resorting to physical violence. The customer lost no time telling the president that he was going to take the policeman's advice and immediately file a complaint if something was not worked out to his satisfaction. He left the bank with a letter from the loan officer stating that no charges would be lodged regarding the assault, along with a new loan agreement that was for the same principal amount as before, except now the interest rate was 1½ percent less than that for the original loan. This change amounted to $510 less that the couple would have to pay back. In return for this consideration, the customer gave the bank a letter stating that he would not pursue the matter regarding the loan, and he returned the original copy of the loan agreement. Here was a guy who made a serious error by resorting to violence, and not only did he get away with it, he also saved $510 in the process! Was he just lucky? Yes, to some extent, but who bears the ultimate responsibility for the entire matter in the first place? The bank does, most certainly. The customer got away with his act and saved money in the exchange because the bank knew it was guilty of questionable business practices. You might not be so lucky, but this is one more case of a mistreated customer saying he was not going to stand for the bank's intimidation. He fought back and won.

The first two examples are, to say the least, unusual. In each case the actions of the customer were both extreme and wrong, even though they won their battles. This next situation is more typical in terms of bank vs. customer, with the customer still obtaining the desired results.

A female customer planning to leave on vacation entered her bank and made a deposit of $2,000 at the teller's window. Realizing she didn't have one of the printed deposit slips encoded with her account number, she asked the teller for a blank deposit slip. Unfortunately, she couldn't remember her account number, and this prompted her to ask the teller to locate the number and print it on the deposit slip. The teller willingly did so, but in her hastiness she copied the wrong account number onto the slip, and the deposit was credited to someone else's account. Needless to say, while the customer who made the deposit was away on vacation, a number of her checks were returned for insufficient funds. The bank officer who sent the checks back did try to call the woman on the phone. He knew her as a good customer who had never been previously overdrawn. Not being successful in reaching her, he felt obligated to return the checks. This problem went on for two weeks, and the number of returned checks steadily escalated. The returned checks included the customer's gas and electric bills, her mortgage payment, etc. Of course, when the woman returned home from her trip she was deluged with overdraft notices from the bank. Also, she began receiving angry phone calls from businesses and individuals who had received her "bad" checks. To make matters even worse, she had been assessed more than $100 in overdraft charges by the bank. She immediately went down to the bank to investigate the problem. The bank officer told her that he would have to look into the matter, and that would take some time. By the following day he had determined what had happened. He called the customer and explained the situation, offering to credit her account for the overdraft charges. Also, the correct deposit amount would be credited as soon as it was collected from the other party who had received the benefit of the deposit. The woman told the banker that she wanted her money *immediately,* and she wanted the bank to write a letter to every party who had received one of her checks, explaining that the error was the bank's and not hers. The officer told her he couldn't write such a letter because it was not bank policy, and it would definitely take a few days to recoup her money. What he neglected to tell her was that the customer who had received the deposit in error had closed out his account, taking all of the $2,000 deposit. The banker knew he would need to retrieve that money before crediting the woman's account. It took the customer almost a week to get her money back into her account, and this was accomplished only after numerous phone calls and persistent visits by her to the bank. The bank finally did what it should have done in the first place, but it still refused to help the woman resolve the credit problem created by the returned checks. Approximately a month later, the woman stopped complaining to the bank's management (she was getting nowhere). She also stopped coming into the bank. Management breathed a sign of relief, however briefly. A few days passed, and then the bank president noticed the customer out in front of the banking office. It appeared that she had been there for some time and seemed to be talking to customers as they entered the bank. As a matter of fact, she was handing the customers something. The president went to one of the customers he knew and asked what was happening. The customer handed him a copy of a complete description of what had happened to the woman standing outside. It contained all the gruesome details of her ordeal. The write-up made it clear who was at fault, how the woman had had to wait a week for her money, and how the bank had refused to help her clarify the matter with her creditors. The president was furious and called the police. After speaking with the woman, the policeman felt she was not obstructing the bank's business and certainly not preventing the customers from entering the bank. The police told the president there was nothing he could do, since she was not breaking any law. The bank's attorney was then contacted. After hearing what the woman had written, the lawyer asked the president if all of it was true. The president reluctantly admitted that it was accurate. The lawyer suggested that the president call in the customer to see if some arrangement could be made to entice her to relinquish her crusade. The president did just that. During the conversation, the woman made it clear that she would continue her Saturday vigils outside the bank until every customer was made aware of the unprofessionalism of the bank's staff. In addition, she had every intention of contacting the local newspapers as soon as possible. The president, who had been ready to have the customer thrown in jail, was now most conciliatory. He told her that the bank would agree to write letters of explanation to all parties who had received one of her checks. He was extremely apologetic for the bank's error and the inconvenience she had been caused. The customer was not completely satisfied. She felt it was going to take more than that to resolve the situation. She countered with the following: (1) She wanted all the letters written to her creditors, (2) she wanted a free checking account, a free safe-deposit box, and some other bank services at no cost to her, and (3) she wanted a part-time job at the bank for her teenage daughter. All her conditions were met. Her daughter is still working at the bank, several years later, with a full-time position. I'm not sure if her daughter knows how or why she obtained the job at the bank, but she is a good employee and treats customers with a great deal of respect.

In each of these cases, the customers decided that the bank's attitude was not appropriate, and they reacted in a positive manner, although in two cases the customers used less than admirable methods. Each customer was able to *negotiate*. Banks rely on the belief that their word is law and that people generally will do whatever they are told. In terms of banking relationships, they generally lose money or suffer the embarrassment of being taken advantage of in these situations. This is not always necessary, because banks *can* be handled if the customer can be just a bit intimidating. It will make you feel better personally and most definitely will make you wealthier. It's neither fun nor profitable being a pawn.

CONCLUSION: AND A BIT MORE INSIDE INFORMATION

It's been my intention to show you how you can successfully beat your bank at its own game. Unfortunately, I can't provide an example of every situation you'll encounter. The important thing is to be aware of what's happening in every transaction.

I could tell you many other ways to beat your bank, but you would be breaking the law, and there lies the problem. If a bank does the same thing to you, it's called "prudent banking practices." If you do it, you'll be in court before you know it. Many of you may wonder at this statement. Surely banks don't really break the law, and if they did, the government would step in and protect the best interests of the public at large, right? Unfortunately, this couldn't be farther from the truth.

The general public must understand, *and soon* if this economic democracy is to survive, that the government will do whatever is necessary to preserve the banking institution as a protected entity, and it does so for one very simple reason: The government needs banks to keep the government's house of cards intact. Every day the government has to borrow billions of dollars to finance its deficits. This becomes a necessity, because it can't afford to finance the national debt with $25 savings bonds. So they sell U.S. agencies in $100,000 blocks, or in larger denominations. And for that the government needs the banks to collect your money so it can borrow from the banks. Without the banking industry as the "front man," the government would have to admit it is broke. Granted, this is an overly simplistic explanation of the "marriage" of the government and the banking industry. However, it gives a rough idea of where our legislators' interests lie. Many laws are made solely to cement the banking industry's hold over this country. For those who doubt this, I would ask why the top ten banks in the country virtually never pay any taxes. I would ask why the banking industry, as a whole, averages approximately a corporate tax payment of 2 percent. They make billions of dollars in income and pay almost no taxes. How does this compare to the typical family of four who are in the 35 percent tax bracket? Wouldn't this indicate that the deck is stacked?

I'm not against free enterprise; that couldn't be farther from the truth. Banks are not part of the free-enterprise system. While the liberals cry about big business and its ability to generate profits, they forget that corporations have a risk factor that morally allows them to earn as much as they can. In fact, the corporation's job is to maximize those earnings if top management is to retain their positions. Banks, on the other hand, have *no* risk factor. What other business can you name that takes your money, makes money on your money, and then charges you for the privilege of letting them use *your* investment? I'm not talking about the interest they charge you on loans. I'm talking about the interest they pay you for your deposits. When the bank pays you interest, it is, in effect, charging you as they discount the monies they made with your money and pay you less than they really earned. For example, let's assume you deposit $25,000 in a time certificate. The bank then loans the same money to three different people to purchase automobiles, except they charge the loan customers 18 percent—not a bad profit for being nothing more than a middleman. If you opened a store and tried to do the same thing a bank does, you would be jailed. Having a charter allows banks to operate in this way.

Let's digress for a moment to show you how the government immediately pounces on anyone attempting to call themselves a bank if they're not part of the banking fraternity. Recently, as a school project, a group of children opened a "bank" as a learning experience. The teacher went to a local bank to obtain information on how it operated so she could guide her students. The bank that she went to subsequently was visited by the bank examiners. It so happened that one of the examiners accidentally saw a note on one of the bank officer's desks referring to the children's "bank." That afternoon the examiners visited the school and told the teacher that the "bank" would have to cease because the students couldn't operate a bank since it was against the law. Think about the implications of the examiners' actions. Clearly, the government is the watchdog of the banking industry— so much so that they would attack a group of schoolchildren who were simply trying to learn the banking system! These are the same examiners, mind you, who sat back and watched over forty individual banks close in 1982. These are the examiners (headed by the Comptroller of the Currency) who not too long ago had to testify on Capitol Hill that the comptroller knew of the problems with the Penn Square Bank in Oklahoma over two years before it closed. The reason a situation like Penn Square can exist is that the government's regulation offices are not there to regulate, but to perpetuate a problem.

How powerful is the banking lobby? Look at the recent reversal of the withholding provision of bank interest paid to depositors. The bottom line was that banks were to withhold quarterly 10 percent of the interest you earned during that quarter. This was intended to speed up the government's ability to collect taxes and supposedly to catch cheaters who were not paying the tax on interest income.

When the banking industry realized that the withholding provision was going to become law, bankers started one of the most insidious campaigns this nation has ever seen. And it was accomplished with your help. Many congressmen stated that they had never received so much mail on any single issue, including the Vietnam War. Mail poured in regarding the withholding issue. The bankers enlisted your help by lying to you, through word of mouth and advertising. If any company misrepresented a product such as banks misrepresented this issue, they would be sued by consumer groups for false advertising. But this was the banking lobby in action. First the banks had to convince the general public that this was a *new* tax when, in fact, it was not. It was a prepayment of taxes you would have owed anyway. A savings account would have lost only about $5 for a balance of $5,000 paying 5.25 percent interest, and only because you would have lost the additional interest on the 10 percent of the interest paid during the quarter. Next, the banks had to convince the elderly that they would suffer the most, since they were on fixed incomes. In fact, most elderly investors would have been completely exempt from the deduction. The banks stressed that they were against it only because they had the best interests of depositors in mind. Nothing could have been farther from the truth.

Why, then, would the banks have objected if they weren't concerned for you? First it would have meant a great deal of extra paperwork for the banks—computer software programs, generating exemptions, generating accountability for forwarding payments to the treasury, etc. Banks don't like to spend money doing anything that doesn't directly reflect on the bank's bottom-line profit picture, and that includes any nonprofitable service to the government. Most of all, the banks didn't want to lose the float on the 10 percent withholding they would have had to send directly to Washington. Although the actual cost to an individual depositor was extremely small (and again, people who haven't been paying their rightful taxes would have been caught in this system), the potential loss of float income to the banking system was enormous, and banks don't easily relinquish their "right" to make additional money with someone else's investment, not even Uncle Sam's. For example, a small $10 million bank would have lost the use of approximately $35,000 in float monies that would not have been available to invest during the year. Using the prime rate of 20 percent, this means that this small bank would have lost $7,000. Not really that much, is it? It is if you realize that a $10 million bank would be termed "high performance" if it made $100,000 in net profits. This means that the proposed withholding provision would have represented 7 percent loss in net income to this bank. Project this 7 percent to a larger institution of $1 billion, and what a monumental eye-opener we have! The loss, in this instance, would amount to a staggering $700,000! Multiply this by the total of all deposits in banks throughout the country and you start to get an idea of why the banks *really* worked so hard to get around the law. The banks once again showed us that they are not to be trusted. They will do whatever they have to, including making you a pawn, in maintaining the industry's power base.

A number of recent banking changes have been applauded by Congress, bankers, and the public. It is not possible to go into each of the new banking services, but it is important to use one example to underscore exactly what is happening. The most significant banking change is the payment of interest on demand deposits (checking accounts). Banks have adopted a number of generic names for these particular accounts, but they are generally referred to as NOW accounts. This account was originally conceived by savings and loan associations to compete more favorably with banks at a time when S&L's were not allowed by law to offer checking accounts. Banks were, until recently, forbidden to pay interest on checking account deposits. Congress, after many decades of making laws partial to the banks, was forced by public opinion to reverse its position. Until this dramatic change, banks were making billions of dollars on the free checking account deposits, and then the roof collapsed. The public woke up, demanding a return on the checking account deposits. Congress responded, and the law was changed. Legislators hailed the new law as a landmark for the average family. Small banks screamed, and the big banks licked their chops. The larger banks knew this was a prime opportunity to break the backs of the smaller competition. Big banks could afford the immediate loss, and in the grand scheme of things felt that the total number of banks would diminish over the next decade. All the bankers sharpened their pencils and earnestly figured how to turn a liability into an asset. The solution turned out to be almost too simple. First let's look at the average way to compute the cost of a checking account prior to the recent changes:

Minimum average balance to receive a free account	$ 300.00
Monthly service charge if not free	1.00
Cost per check ($.03 each), 20 checks written	.60
NSF charge ($5.00 each), 1 returned	5.00
Stop payment ($5.00 each), 1 this month	5.00
Total	$ 11.60

This may not represent a typical month, but we're going to compare the same account transactions with the new interest-bearing account. With the account not paying interest all your checks were returned to you. In the next example they are not, and if you want a copy of a particular check it would cost you $2 for each request.

Now we enter the new era of interest-bearing checking accounts. This, after all, is what we've all been waiting for, right? No more will banks get to use our money free. They have to pay us interest. Boy, what a deal! Or is it? Let's take a closer look.

Minimum average balance to receive a free account	$ 400.00
Monthly service charge if not free	5.00
Cost per check ($.05 each), 20 checks written	1.00
NSF charge ($10.00 each), 1 returned	10.00
Stop payment ($10.00 each), 1 this month	10.00

Check retrieval request (copy of checks no longer returned with statement) ($2.00 each), 2 copies needed	4.00
Minus interest earned at 5.25%	(1.31)
Average balance for month = $300.00	
Total	$ 28.69

The banks increased *all* their service charges when this new banking law went into effect. This was the chance they had been waiting for. With the help of Congress, banks managed to charge the customer $17.09 *more* for the privilege of receiving interest on a checking account. To be fair to the banks, you typically wouldn't use all the services listed in these tables every month. So let's alter the example, leaving only the basics of a $300.00 average balance account with twenty checks written per month. Computed in the old way, your exposure to a charge amounts to $1.60. The new method costs $4.69.

There are, of course, a number of other examples that bankers would use to indicate that the customer is making money with the new approach. They might cite the customer with a balance of $3,000 in a checking account. This customer, hardly typical, would receive a net return of $13.12. In this case, the banker would be telling the truth. What he or she is failing to say, however, is that affluent people don't keep high balances in their checking accounts. They would never have become affluent that way. Affluent people have their money working elsewhere, and while they may have $3,000 in a checking account, it is proportionately smaller when compared to their total net worth. In addition, banks resort to extensive marketing research to measure *exactly* what the average account at the bank is. After isolating the greatest volume range, they establish the balance requirements higher so the vast majority of customers have to pay a monthly service charge. Don't think that the bank picks those service charges out of a hat. The bottom line here, as always, is that banks have figured a way to beat you out of your money. And you have again become the victim.

It may appear at the conclusion of this book that I am being awfully hard on banks and bankers, but I've told the truth. Banks have *no* interest in you whatsoever. And the trend is getting worse. Recently, a major New York bank changed its service policy (and I use the term "service policy" loosely). Customers with a balance in their account of less than $5,000 would not be permitted to use a teller. They would have to stand in line and use a teller machine. The more affluent customers could walk right in and approach a teller's window with no waiting in line. These are the same considerate people who want you to believe they are concerned for your welfare, and the issue of 10 percent withholding on your savings interest. It seems hypocritical to me, but you be the judge.

Many bankers have told me that their objective with the new changes in the law was to lose a certain percentage of their customer base—they couldn't afford to service the small balance accounts, and they would just as soon be rid of them by imposing extremely high service charges.

Even though I have made strong accusations against the banking industry, I must state again that banks are public corporations. As such they have certain rights and privileges. They are obligated to their shareholders to make money and show a reasonable profit. I have no objection to this until I evaluate all the ramifications and overall intent of the banking system. Banks are granted their charter providing they can demonstrate a need within the community for their services. They are obligated, by law, to provide certain services to the public. Morally, they are also obligated to service the legitimate needs of depositors. Yet banks have been granted unbelievable special concessions from the government. They are a monopoly of gigantic proportions. They have a stranglehold on the very financial freedom they are expected to promote and protect. And they do it with the help of your congressman and senators.

Where does all this put you? It's no secret that the responsibility for your family's financial future lies directly on your shoulders. You must search for the few banks that are truly dedicated to serving the community. Even at that, you must continually fight to gain concessions in your banking relationships. Learn all you can about a particular account, finding out how the bank computes the interest on that savings account or on that NOW account. "A little learning is a dangerous thing," and in this case the saying is very true. Your banker isn't smarter than you are. Investigate all the local financial institutions in your area. Maybe one bank's checking account is better than another, while one may have a better way of computing the interest on savings accounts. You may find a bank with lower rates for safe-deposit boxes, and hours more convenient to your needs. I could go on, but you get the message: *It's up to you!* You're now armed and ready to do battle!

GLOSSARY

ACTIVE ACCOUNT: In banking, an account where deposits and withdrawals are frequently made.

ACTIVITY CHARGE: The service charge on a depositor's account. These vary greatly from bank to bank.

ADMINISTRATOR: A person appointed by the court to settle the estate of one who died without a will.

AFFILIATE BANK: A bank whose management is closely associated with another bank or financial institution.

AMERICAN BANKERS ASSOCIATION: The ABA is the national organization of banks. The vast majority of banks belong to the ABA.

AMERICAN INSTITUTE OF BANKING: The educational extension of the ABA.

AMORTIZATION LOANS: A term that applies to long-term loans (such as a mortgage) in which the principal borrowed is paid off over the period of the loan.

APPRAISAL: The act of putting a value (fair market or loan value) on a piece of property.

APPRAISER: The person who completes the appraisal.

APPRECIATION: The increase in the value of property as compared to cost.

177

ASSETS: A term used to signify properties of any kind that have a value and are owned by an individual or business.

AUTHORIZED CAPITAL STOCK: The number of shares of stock that a bank is authorized to issue as outlined by its banking charter.

AVERAGE DAILY BALANCE: The balance of an account added together for thirty days and then divided by thirty. This gives the bank a starting point when figuring the profitability of an account.

BAD DEBTS: Those accounts of the bank that are charged off and represent an actual monetary loss of funds to a bank. This can result from a bad loan, a bank error, or other circumstances.

BALLOON PAYMENT: A payment due in the future that is larger than the regular monthly payment. This type of payment is used most often with mortgage lending.

BANK ACCOUNT: Monies deposited in a bank. These are generally checking accounts, savings accounts, and time certificates of deposit.

BANK BALANCE: The amount deposited in a bank in your name that you are entitled to draw against.

BANK BYLAWS: The rules by which an individual bank is managed. Such bylaws cannot be inconsistent with appropriate banking laws and the bank's charter.

BANK EXAMINERS: Persons appointed by law to examine the financial affairs of a banking institution.

BANK LENDING RISK: The business risk that is present in an institution that lends monies. The percentage of risk is determined by the expertise of the bank managers.

BANK MONEY ORDER: A money order issued by a bank that is paid for in advance. The cost is usually minimal.

BANKRUPT: A financial condition of a person or business unable to meet their financial obligations and has been declared by a court to be discharged from further payments incurred before the bankruptcy.

BANKS: In general terms, a corporation legally organized to provide deposit facilities to the general public and businesses.

BANK STAMP: The endorsement of a bank placed on the reverse side of a check indicating acceptance and payment.

BEARER: The person in possession of a negotiable instrument made payable to the individual presenting the instrument.

BENEFICIARY: The person for whose benefit a trust account operates.

BLANK ENDORSEMENT: An endorsement with no specific payee and may be paid by signature to the bearer.

BOOK VALUE: The value of bank stock as shown by the bank's records. This is the bank's total capital stock, capital surplus, undivided profits, and legal reserves divided by the number of bank shares outstanding.

BORROWER: A person to whom money is loaned.

BRANCH BANKING: The system of banking that allows a bank to do business in multiple locations other than its main office only.

BUDGET: The estimated income and expense of an individual or business.

CALL REPORT: The statement of condition of a bank, as prepared by order of the appropriate governmental agency. A condensed version of this report must be made public through newspaper publication.

CANCELED CHECK: A check received with your monthly statement and that has been paid and canceled by the bank.

CAPITAL AND SURPLUS: In a general sense, a condensed accounting indicating a bank's financial strength.

CAPITAL STOCK: The stock of a bank that has been issued in return for the payment of investment monies from its shareholders.

CASHIER'S CHECK: A bank check that can be purchased that becomes a direct obligation of the bank.

CASH ITEMS: Checks, drafts, etc., that are deposited for immediate credit but are subject to reversal should they be returned.

CERTIFICATE OF DEPOSIT: A receipt for a deposit either payable on demand, or at a predetermined date by mutual agreement between the bank and the customer. Generally, a form of savings account.

CERTIFIED CHECK: A check that guarantees that the signature of the drawer is genuine and that there are sufficient funds on deposit to pay the check. Payment cannot be refused due to insufficient funds.

CHECK: A bill of exchange drawn on a bank and payable on demand.

CHECKING ACCOUNT: A bank account against which the checks may be drawn.

CHRISTMAS CLUB: A savings account with weekly deposits, the balance of which is payable in December.

COLLATERAL LOAN: A loan for which the borrower has pledged collateral security and that may be sold by the lender if the loan conditions are not met.

COLLECTED BALANCE: The balance in an account that the bank has actually been paid for. This collected balance is always less than your book balance.

COLLECTION ITEMS: Deposits in a bank for which credit is given the depositor only when the items have actually been paid for at the payee bank.

COMMON STOCK: That part of the bank's stock distinguished from preferred stock. Common stock represents the last claim on assets.

COMPENSATING BALANCES: Deposits in a demand account that a bank requires on certain commercial loans, usually 20 percent of the outstanding loan balance.

COUNTER CHECK: A check available to bank customers that takes the place of their own check if one is not available.

DEBENTURE: Bonds issued by a bank that are unsecured by any specific bank asset.

DEFALCATION: The fraudulent appropriation by a bank employee of bank monies or properties.

DEFAULT: The failure to meet a lending obligation or the terms as stated in the lending contract.

DEMAND DEPOSITS: Deposits subject to check and that can be withdrawn immediately, without notice to the bank.

DEMAND LOAN: A loan that is payable at demand by the lender.

DEPOSITS: Monies owed by a bank to its depositors.

DIRECTORS: A group of individuals who have the direct responsibility of bank management.

DIVIDEND: A proportionate distribution of a bank's earnings to its shareholders.

DRAWEE: The bank at which a check is expected to be paid.

DRAWER: The person who makes out the check.

EARNINGS PER SHARE: The bank's yearly earnings divided by the number of shares outstanding.

EMBEZZLEMENT: The fraudulent appropriation of monies entrusted to a bank under a fiduciary relationship.

ENDORSEMENT: The writing by the payee on the back of a check or other negotiable instrument. The signature and delivery of the item pass title to another individual.

EQUITY: The difference between the market value of a property and the amount still owed on the property.

EXECUTOR: A person appointed via a will to carry out the wishes of the deceased.

FDIC: Federal Depositors Insurance Corporation, an executive agency that insures deposits for all banks entitled to FDIC insurance.

FEDERAL FUNDS: Funds on deposit at a Federal Reserve bank by member banks. This is the principal source for daily investments by banks.

FEDERAL RESERVE BANK:Any one of the twelve Federal Reserve banks established under the Federal Reserve Act.

FIDUCIARY: A person or corporation (bank) that is entrusted with the property of another, subject to the specifics of the trust instrument.

FIFO: An acronym meaning First In-First Out. For purpose of interest computation the bank considers any withdrawal to come out of the earliest deposit or balance during the interest period. This is more costly to the depositor than LIFO or daily interest.

FINANCIAL STATEMENT: Another term for balance sheet, statement of condition, etc.

FIRST LIEN: The first right or claim against a property such as a home or other pledged collateral.

FLOAT: The funds deposited that received immediate credit and have yet to be collected by the receiving bank.

FORECLOSURE: Action taken by the mortgageholder when the conditions of a mortgage have not been met. The mortgageholder may institute legal proceedings to force the owner to pay the mortgage in full or sell the property.

FORGED NEGOTIABLE INSTRUMENT: Checks, etc., with the makers or the payee's signature having been falsified. Also refers to alteration of a document for the purpose of defrauding.

GARNISHMENT: A legal process authorizing a bank (or others) to impound monies on deposit for the purpose of paying another debt. The bank awaits the decision of the court before paying such a debt.

GUARANTEE: A promise to pay in case of default.

GUARANTOR: A person who guarantees payment of a loan to a bank even though the person did not receive the benefits of the monies.

GUARDIAN: A person who has the legal right to control a minor or the estate of another.

HOLDER IN DUE COURSE: A person who takes a negotiable instrument (1) for value, (2) in good faith, (3) without prior knowledge that the instrument is defective in any way.

INACTIVE ACCOUNT: A banking account where little or no activity occurs. These accounts are normally segregated from active accounts and are oftentimes assessed service charges until the remaining balance is absorbed.

INSTALLMENT LOAN: A loan whereby the customer pays a portion of the value of the loan each month until the amount owed is completely amortized.

INSUFFICIENT FUNDS: A banking term denoting the return of a check because the depositor does not have a balance sufficient enough to allow the item to be paid.

INTEREST: The "rental" cost of money paid by the bank to its depositors or paid by loan customers for the privilege of borrowing money from the bank.

INTERLOCKING DIRECTORS: Directors of one bank who are also directors of another bank.

JOINT ACCOUNT: A bank account owned by two or more individuals.

JOINT TENANCY: Property owned by two or more people by title.

JUNIOR MORTGAGE: A lower-ranking mortgage as distinguished from a first mortgage.

KITING: A banking term that denotes the raising of fictitious balances on uncollected funds among a number of financial institutions or individuals.

LIABILITIES: The obligations of a person or business.

LIEN: The right to hold property as a pledge against a loan.

LIFO: An acronym meaning last in, first out. For purpose of interest computation the bank considers any withdrawal to come out of the latest deposit or balance during the interest period. This is more costly to the depositor than daily interest but is better than FIFO.

LINE OF CREDIT: The maximum that a person can borrow from a bank with prior approval from the institution.

LIQUID ASSETS: Current assets that can readily be converted to cash.

LOANS: The renting of money to be repaid with interest.

LOST PASSBOOK: This is not a serious matter, since a passbook is only a memorandum of deposits. A lost passbook should be reported to the bank as soon as possible.

MAKER: A person who writes out a check.

MARKET VALUE: The current salable value of a property.

MATURITY: The due date of a financial obligation.

MINIMUM FREE BALANCE: The minimum account balance allowed for the customer to receive a free checking account.

MINUTES: The written proceedings of a board or shareholders' meeting.

MONEY: A medium of exchange.

MONEY MARKET: In a general sense, the supply of funds and the demand for said funds.

MONEY ORDER: A negotiable instrument calling for the payment of monies to another and paid for in advance by the purchaser. Usually purchased by people who do not have checking accounts.

MORTGAGE: The note that conveys title to land that is used for collateral for a mortgageholder (bank).

NEGOTIABLE INSTRUMENTS: Orders, or promises, to pay

money. Payable by endorsement and delivery. A check is a negotiable instrument.

NET WORTH: The value of a person's estate after deducting all outstanding obligations. If the obligations exceed the worth of all the person's property, a negative net worth is created.

NSF: An acronym for nonsufficient funds.

OBLIGOR: A debtor, a person who owes money.

OVERDRAFT: An account on the books of a bank that indicates the total of all the customers who have overdrawn their accounts.

OVEREXTENSION: A condition whereby a person owes more debt than he or she can reasonably be expected to pay.

PASSBOOK: A book that records deposits and withdrawals made at a bank.

PAYEE: A person to whom a check is made payable.

PERSONAL CHECK: A check made out by a person as opposed to a business.

PERSONAL PROPERTY: All property that belongs to a person that is not real property (land).

POSTDATED CHECK: A check that bears a date that has not yet arrived.

POWER OF ATTORNEY: A document that allows one person to act in the name of another.

PRIME RATE: The interest rate that is charged for those loans presenting the least risk to a bank.

PRINCIPAL: The face value of a note.

PROMISSORY NOTE: A note that indicates that one person will pay another, or a bank, certain monies at a predetermined future date.

REAL ESTATE:The term for real property.

REFER TO MAKER: A method of returning a check that tells the payee to ask the maker of the check why the check was not honored. It is a bank's way of not becoming involved in the transaction.

RENEWAL: The extension of a loan note by a bank allowing the customer to "pay off" the old note and replacing it with a new note.

REPURCHASE AGREEMENT: A note sold by a bank to a customer, with the obligation to repurchase at a later date by the bank.

RETURNED ITEM: A check returned from the drawee bank to the presenting bank due to an irregularity.

SAVINGS ACCOUNTS: Those funds on deposit at a bank that earn interest and are not subject to a check withdrawal.

SAVINGS BANKS: Banks whose express purpose it is to promote savings by individuals.

SECOND MORTGAGE: A mortgage placed on real property that already has a first mortgage against it.

SECURED LOAN: A loan wherein the lender has some collateral pledged by the borrower in case of default.

SECURITY: A pledge of property as loan collateral.

SHORT-TERM LOANS: Loans having a maturity of less than one year.

SIGHT DRAFT: A draft payable on presentation.

SIGNATURES: A bank is obligated to know the signatures of its depositors and is liable if it pays an instrument with a forged signature.

STATEMENT OF ACCOUNT: A record prepared by a bank and sent to a customer that outlines all transactions during a given period.

STOCK CERTIFICATE: A certificate of partial ownership of a bank.

STOCKHOLDER: The owner of one or more shares of bank stock.

STOP PAYMENT: The order from a depositor to a bank not to honor a specific check.

TELLER: A bank employee who accepts deposits and honors withdrawals from customers.

THIRD MORTGAGE: A mortgage placed on real property that already has a first and a second mortgage against it.

TIME DEPOSIT: Deposit due to a customer at a specified future time. This is a form of savings account and may take many different forms, with different interest rates based on the length of the contract.

TITLE: Evidence that a party is the rightful owner of a piece of property.

TRAVELER'S CHECKS: Checks sold by banks and that often

are honored worldwide. They are drawn on a different corporation than the bank.

TREASURY BILLS: Noninterest-bearing notes issued by the U.S. government. They are sold at a discounted rate and redeemed at face value.

TRUST: The preservation of property so that an individual may benefit from the resulting income.

TRUST DEPARTMENT: The department of a bank that deals in trust business.

TRUSTEE: A person to whom a trust is committed.

UNENCUMBERED: Property free of all claims.

UNSECURED LOAN: A loan having collateral or security.

U.S. GOVERNMENT SECURITIES: Financial obligations of the United States government.

USURY: Loan interest in excess of the legal maximum.

WIRE TRANSFER: The transfer of money verbally by phone as opposed to transfer by a negotiable instrument.

INDEX